THE BIG BOOK OF CANADA

Lucius O'Brien, View of the Rockies, *1887*.

THE BIG BOOK OF CANADA

Illustrations by Bill Slavin

CHRISTOPHER MOORE

Introduction by Janet Lunn

Tundra Books

Text copyright © 2002 by Christopher Moore Editorial Ltd.
Illustrations copyright © 2002 by Bill Slavin
Introduction copyright © 2002 by Janet Lunn

Published in Canada by Tundra Books,
481 University Avenue, Toronto, Ontario M5G 2E9

Published in the United States by Tundra Books of Northern New York,
P.O. Box 1030, Plattsburgh, New York 12901

Library of Congress Control Number: 2002101971

The poem on p. 207 is copyright © 1907 by Robert W. Service.
It is used by permission of Wm. Krasilovsky, Agent, New York.

National Library of Canada Cataloguing in Publication Data

Moore, Christopher
The big book of Canada : exploring the provinces and territories

Includes bibliographical references and index.
ISBN 0-88776-457-6

1. Canada – Juvenile literature. 2. Canada – Geography – Juvenile literature. I. Slavin, Bill II. Title.

We acknowledge the support of the Canada Council for the Arts
and the Ontario Arts Council for our publishing program.

We acknowledge the financial support of the Government of Canada through
the Book Publishing Industry Development Program for our publishing activities.

Project Management: Janice Weaver
Additional Editing: Barbara Hehner
Design: Terri Nimmo

Printed and bound in Canada

1 2 3 4 5 6   07 06 05 04 03 02

This is for Kate
– C. M.

For Fernando
– B. S.

Confederation Conference, 1864.

CONTENTS

INTRODUCTION

Janet Lunn

I f you travel across Canada over many years, visiting all the provinces and territories, you begin to see the country the way you do a city: as a collection of neighbourhoods with personalities that have developed from the individual characteristics of the land and the people who have settled there. These neighbourhoods are as different from one another as are local neighbourhoods in Toronto, Montreal, Halifax, Saskatoon, Winnipeg, or Vancouver. How very different Newfoundland and Saskatchewan, Ontario and British Columbia are from one another, and yet they make a whole that is definitely Canada, a Canada we all recognize and share in. Wherever you go in this country, you will find people who tell you they feel a connection to the Arctic landscape that hovers over all of us, that they delight in the humour of the Newfoundlanders, that they consider Anne of Green Gables to be alive and well in their own province, and that Ontario's Group of Seven painted this country just for them. And yet Newfoundland humour, *Anne of Green Gables*, and the Group of Seven do belong to very separate and distinct places. This atlas-size book is not intended to be a comprehensive geography or history of the country. Instead, it is a kind of gazetteer of Canada's provinces and territories. Christopher Moore is well known for his knack of ferreting out fascinating and little-known facts and stories to highlight his historical works, and here he has put these facts and stories front and centre to create a compendium of informative and entertaining chapters about Canada's ten provinces and three territories.

With the help of both modern and archival photographs and Bill Slavin's charming illustrations, *The Big Book of Canada* becomes everything a good gazetteer should be. There is, in each chapter, a map of the province, a brief description of its geography and history, biographical sketches of a few famous sons and daughters (past and present), a timeline of important events, and even a recipe of a local culinary specialty. And then there are those quirky bits that we all treasure about the places we live in, visit, or just read about. The Newfoundland chapter includes a brief glossary of words not common in the rest of Canada. In the chapter on Nova Scotia, you learn that the woman who inspired the musical *The King and I* once lived there, and that they delight in a dessert called blueberry grunt. And that's just the beginning. You'll also discover that some of New Brunswick's rivers are privately owned, that most of Ontario's first-class farmland is visible from the top of the CN Tower in Toronto, that Alberta was named for the daughter of Queen Victoria who was married to the governor general of Canada at the time the province joined Confederation, that there are more First Nations languages in British Columbia than in all the rest of Canada, and that the coldest winter temperature ever registered in the country was in Snag, Yukon, in 1947 (−63°C!).

The Big Book of Canada is filled to overflowing with facts and stories just like these – little-known pieces of information that celebrate the individual character of each one of our provinces and territories and make it easy to see how they came to be as they are today. They also explain what makes this beautiful and amazing country feel like home to all of us, wherever we live.

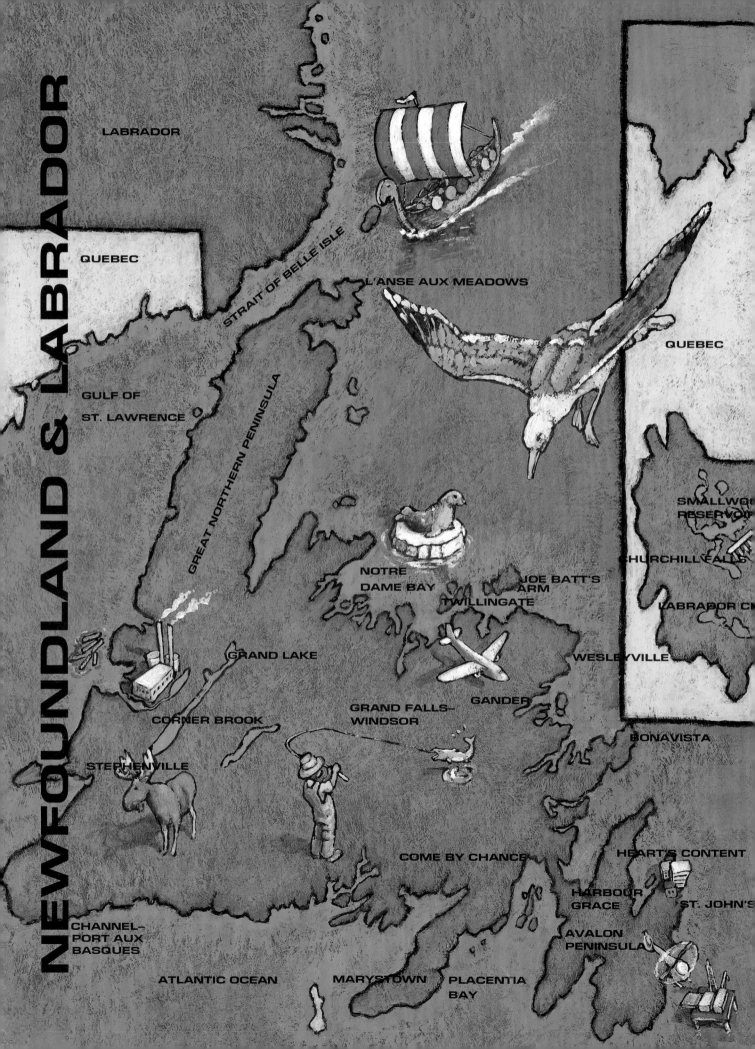

RAMAH

ATLANTIC OCEAN

NAIN

DAVIS INLET

HOPEDALE

MAKKOVIK

LAKE MELVILLE

RED BAY

BY GREAT WATERS

The rugged, rocky coasts of Newfoundland and Labrador, scoured by ice, pounded by the stormy Atlantic, loom up out of the fog. Over the centuries, Beothuk canoeists, Viking explorers, Basque and French and English fishers, outport sealers, and the crews of modern supertankers have all responded to these shores with respect and awe.

The people of Newfoundland and Labrador have had to be as tough and resilient as the ancient, weathered rocks they live on. For five hundred years, these people lived by and from the sea. They saw themselves as Newfoundlanders, and only recently became Canadians as well. Newfoundland is the newest Canadian province.

"Come here at your peril, Canadian wolf," Newfoundlanders sang as they turned down Confederation in the 1860s. They did not join Canada until a man named Joseph Smallwood led them in 1949. Since then, Newfoundland has changed a lot. Fewer Newfoundlanders now live in the hundreds of small, isolated outports along the coast. Lumbering, oil wells, and electric power dams have all become important industries. In the 1990s, the fishing industry, once Newfoundland's chief livelihood, fell into crisis, and most fishing had to stop.

Newfoundland's great challenge – to improve its citizens' opportunities and living standards – continues. The province needs outside investment, but it also seeks to control its own resources for the benefit of Newfoundlanders. There is a powerful sense of pride and independence in the people of Newfoundland and Labrador. Some argue that the hard, self-sufficient, close-to-nature outport life should still be a part of the province's future.

Most Canadians probably imagine Newfoundland and Labrador as surf pounding on a rocky, fog-shrouded shore. But the province has many landscapes: the mountainous west coast and Great Northern Peninsula; the lakes, rivers, and waterfalls of the Labrador interior; and the forests of central Newfoundland. And there is an undersea "landscape" too, for the Grand Banks have always been a vital part of the province.

THE GRAND BANKS

Some of Newfoundland's most important landscapes lie under water. The Grand Banks are a submerged extension of continental North America. Nearly three times the size of the island itself, the banks are mostly no more than a hundred metres beneath the surface of the ocean. (Just a little farther out, the Atlantic Ocean is five thousand metres deep.)

On the Grand Banks, warm water from the Gulf Stream meets cold water from the Labrador Current. One result is a blanket of fog that conceals the icebergs that float across the banks every spring. The other result is a rich underwater environment, abounding in plankton and therefore in fish, whales, seals, and seabirds. And for five hundred years, fishing boats have been drawn to the banks too. Big factory ships and trawlers arrived only fifty years ago, but there is barely a metre that their bottom-dragging nets have not covered.

THE TORNGAT MOUNTAINS

Rising straight out of the Atlantic along the northern tip of Labrador, the Torngats are the highest part of Canada anywhere east of the Rockies. Between the peaks, deep fjords lead in to glacier-scoured valleys and treeless shorelines. Hunting and trading peoples have long inhabited these lands. At Ramah Bay, they quarried Ramah chert, a precious, almost glass-like stone that was used for blades and tools. For thousands of years, Ramah chert was traded all along North America's Eastern Seaboard.

THE COASTAL HARBOURS

Forty thousand years ago, glaciers carried the soils of Newfoundland out to the Grand Banks, but the hard granite underneath endured. Today the coastlines of Newfoundland and Labrador are a tangle of headlands, cliffs, islands, and inlets carved out by the ice and the surf. Most of the province's people have always lived close to these shores. Fish, shellfish, game, and shelter were readily available, while the sea was a highway to the rest of the island and the rest of the world. In the 1700s, almost every good harbour on the eastern half of Newfoundland became an "outport," home to a few fishing families. Many outports are still there today.

Glaciation made the fjords and finger lakes of the Torngat Mountains.

THE INTERIOR FOREST

When fishers from Europe took over the shorelines of Newfoundland, the Native Beothuk people retreated to the rugged and rolling interior of the island. When William Cormack, one of the few Europeans who tried to save the Beothuk from extinction, walked across Newfoundland in 1822, he found long lakes and rich forests, a world very different from the fog-shrouded coastline. In the twentieth century, lumber and mining towns sprang up across the interior of the island, and the Trans-Canada Highway was built from Port aux Basques to St. John's. This is also where Newfoundlanders and visitors come to hunt moose and deer and to fish in the wild rivers.

MOMENTS

1860s Newfoundland took part in the colonial conferences that produced the new Canadian nation. But the island had been getting along on its own for 250 years by then, and the rest of Canada seemed very far away. Newfoundlanders chose to remain apart from the new nation.

1881 Construction began on a cross-Newfoundland railway.

1914 In one of Newfoundland's most famous disasters at sea, seventy-seven men died out on the open ice while hunting for seals during a blizzard.

1916 The 1st Newfoundland Regiment, the island's fighting force, was nearly wiped out when it was sent to charge the enemy machine guns at Beaumont Hamel, in France, on July 1, the first day of fighting in the First World War's infamous Battle of the Somme.

1934 Debt and depression brought Newfoundland's eighty-two years of self-government to an end. A British body, called the Commission of Government, ran the colony for the next fifteen years.

1949 Canada – yes or no? After the Second World War ended in 1945, Newfoundlanders convened a national convention to debate their future. In 1948, by the narrowest of margins, Newfoundlanders finally voted to become Canadians. Newfoundland became the tenth province at the stroke of midnight on March 31, 1949.

1953 Premier Joseph Smallwood declared that outport life had to cease. For hundreds of years, most Newfoundlanders had lived in isolated communities, without doctors, schools, electricity, roads, or any modern services. Smallwood said they would be better off if they burned their boats, abandoned the outports, and moved to a few larger centres, where jobs and services would be provided for all. Some outport houses were put on barges and floated away to the new centres. Many more were simply locked up and left, beside the abandoned wharves, paths, churches, and cemeteries.

1966 Thirty thousand workers began constructing dams and

Some families took their houses with them when they left their isolated outports.

powerhouses to turn Labrador's Churchill Falls into one of the world's greatest sources of hydroelectric power. But the power travelled to its customers through Quebec, and soon it was Quebec, not Newfoundland, that was earning the most from the sale of Churchill Falls electricity.

1972 Joseph Smallwood, who had led Newfoundland into Confederation and been its premier ever since, lost the provincial election. Joey, as he was commonly called, struggled on in politics for several more years without success. Then he retired to write books about his beloved province.

1982 The *Ocean Ranger*, the largest offshore drill rig in the world, was exploring for oil on the underwater oilfields three hundred kilometres east of St. John's. In the midst of a February Atlantic gale, it suddenly capsized and sank. All eighty-four workers aboard (fifty-six of them Newfoundlanders) were lost.

This battered lifeboat is almost all that was found of the doomed Ocean Ranger.

1985 There was oil under the Grand Banks, and drilling had already begun. But who controlled the oil – Canada or Newfoundland? In 1984, the Supreme Court said Canada did, but in 1985, the Canadian government agreed to share control with Newfoundland.

1990 When islanders say "fish," they mean cod. The cod of the Grand Banks first drew Europeans to Newfoundland, and it kept them coming for five hundred years. But in the twentieth century, fishing technology improved, catches rose, and fleets from more and more nations joined the hunt. Suddenly in 1990, there were no more cod to catch. Fishing had to stop, and Newfoundlanders had to look for other livelihoods. All through the 1990s, scientists and citizens alike wondered, Would the cod ever come back to the Grand Banks?

The Beothuk Demasduit, who died of tuberculosis in 1820.

BEOTHUK

European fishers who first came to Newfoundland took over the shorelines where the Beothuk people of the island had once summered. So the Beothuk and the settlers fought, and the Beothuk people were driven to the rugged interior. Hard-pressed for food and shelter, ravaged by tuberculosis, attacked by raiders, they dwindled in number. The last Beothuk woman died in St. John's in the 1820s. Much of the language – as well as many of the beliefs and stories – of Newfoundland's early people was lost forever.

INNU

The Innu are nomadic caribou hunters who learned to survive and prosper on Labrador's Barren Grounds. In recent years, they have begun to inhabit more permanent settled communities, and the change has been difficult for them. Today the Innu struggle with poverty and social problems as they strive to hand down the skills and traditions of the hunt, and to secure control of their lands through treaties with the federal and provincial governments.

IRISH

Are all Newfoundlanders Irish? No, but it sometimes seems that way. Irish families came to fish and settle in Newfoundland – Talamn an Eisc, in Irish Gaelic – from early times. Irish names, Irish accents, Irish music, and many Irish traditions and customs are a deep part of the life of Newfoundland and Labrador. Many of the outport communities were strongly Irish and Catholic, and the Newfoundland accent still has a strong echo of Irish in it.

WEST COUNTRY ENGLISH

Fishing entrepreneurs from Poole, Dartmouth, and other towns in southwest England built much of Newfoundland's trade in codfish. Newfoundland communities that are not Irish and Catholic usually have Protestant, West Country roots, and many of the merchants of St. John's also came from that part of England.

COME-FROM-AWAY

You are either a Newfoundlander or not. Some islanders have lived forty years in Toronto or Fort McMurray, and they still think of themselves as Newfoundlanders. And the reverse is also true: even if you have lived for decades in Newfoundland, you are still "come from away" if you do not have roots and ancestors on "the Rock."

FIGGY DUFF

Outport people ate a lot of dried, pickled, or preserved food. Figgy duff is a sweet dessert boiled in a can, a traditional favourite so popular that a well-known Newfoundland music group called itself Figgy Duff.

3 cups (750 mL) stale bread
1/4 cup (50 mL) melted butter
1 cup (250 mL) raisins
1 tbsp (15 mL) molasses
1/2 cup (125 mL) brown sugar
1 tsp (5 mL) each ginger, allspice, cinnamon
1 tsp (5 mL) baking soda

salt
1 tbsp (15 mL) hot water
1/2 cup (125 mL) flour

Soak bread in water for a few minutes. Press out water and rub to form breadcrumbs. Do not pack bread tightly when measuring 3 cups (750 mL). Combine bread, raisins, sugar, salt, and spices, and mix with a fork. Add butter, molasses, and baking soda dissolved in hot water. Add flour and mix. Pour into tin can or baking pan. Boil for 1 1/2 hours. Serve with molasses.

ST. JOHN'S

St. John's is one of the oldest cities in North America, and it's still one of the great ones. It is a harbour, a seaport, a capital, and the centre of Newfoundland culture. Outport people have sometimes resented the wealth and power of the "townies," but not much has ever gone on in Newfoundland without going through St. John's. Newfiejohn, sailors used to call it, to distinguish it from Saint John, New Brunswick, or St- Jean, Quebec.

CORNER BROOK

Newfoundland's second-largest city, Corner Brook, which sits at the head of a spectacular fjord called the Humber Arm, is the gateway to western Newfoundland and the Great Northern Peninsula. One of the world's largest pulp mills is the town's economic backbone, and it's buttressed by other resource industries and a branch of Memorial University.

L'ANSE AUX MEADOWS

It used to be called L'Anse aux Méduse (jellyfish bay), and it was an isolated outport on the Strait of Belle Isle, far from the road and the attention of the world. Today, however, L'Anse aux Meadows is a destination that draws many visitors up the Great Northern Peninsula. They come to see the reconstructed remains of the only place where Norse sailors are known to have wintered in North America, about the year 1000 A.D.

L'Anse aux Meadows.

TWILLINGATE

Dorset peoples from the north and Beothuk from Newfoundland came to hunt and fish on this island in Notre Dame Bay, off northeastern Newfoundland. Later came French fishers, who named it Toulinguet, for a town in Brittany. In the 1700s, merchants and fishers from the English West Country replaced the French, and Twillingate became a base for the cod trade and the winter seal hunt. Today it is a regional centre for northeastern Newfoundland, and a causeway links it to the mainland.

GANDER

In the 1950s, Gander was one of the crossroads of the world. Passenger and freight aircraft crossing the Atlantic needed a refuelling stop, and Gander's airport, built for Allied air forces during the Second World War, became a busy stopover for international air traffic. With the arrival of long-distance jets in the 1970s, however, Gander's air traffic declined.

NAIN

For centuries, German missionaries of the Moravian Protestant faith ministered to the Inuit of the north Labrador coast. Most of the missionaries are gone now, but if you sail into Nain, you may still be met at the harbour by an Inuit brass band playing German hymns. Nain has become a population centre for northern Labrador, with schools, a radio station, Inuit organizations, and other services.

SIGNAL HILL

If some giant rolled it over, Signal Hill could plug the harbour or crush the city of St. John's. This bare chunk of stone has guided sailors to the port, and battles have swirled around it several times. In 1901, the Italian inventor Guglielmo Marconi built a radio tower here and sent the first radio signal across the Atlantic.

RED BAY

This Labrador village on the Strait of Belle Isle was founded by fishing families from Conception Bay, Newfoundland, early in the 1800s. But in the 1500s, it was "the world capital of whaling." Each summer, Basque sailors from France and Spain made their headquarters here while they hunted whales in the nearby waters.

CHURCHILL FALLS

Deep in the interior of Labrador, the Churchill River plunges and tumbles down hundreds of metres. Churchill Falls was once a spectacular seventy-five-metre plunge, higher than Niagara Falls. In 1969, however, the falls were silenced by one of the largest hydroelectric developments in the world. Today many Newfoundlanders feel more anger than pride about Churchill Falls. The electricity is sent over power lines through the province of Quebec, which earns vast profits from Labrador's water power while Newfoundland gets little benefit.

St. John's is the foggiest city in Canada (121 days a year) – and the windiest too (average wind speed: 24 kilometres per hour).

By the 1950s, inshore fishermen like these were rarely seen in Newfoundland.

INSHORE FISHERS

Until fifty years ago, all Newfoundland fishing was small scale, done mostly by individual fishers with baited lines. But since about 1950, the Grand Banks have been prowled by ocean-going "draggers" towing deep nets, and by factory ships equipped to process and freeze the catch right on board. This high-technology kind of fishing has almost destroyed the cod stocks of the western Atlantic.

Many Newfoundlanders have struggled to continue their local small-boat fishing, which allows them to be close to nature and always aware of the state of the local fish stocks. Many of them think that this, the oldest Newfoundland fishing industry, is the only one that will survive.

HELICOPTER PILOTS

When the oil industry came to Newfoundland in the 1970s, the off-shore drilling platforms needed regular, timely delivery of crews and supplies. St. John's developed a helicopter industry, and today Newfoundland's helicopter pilots are busy serving oil rigs and other resource industries in Newfoundland and internationally.

CARIBOU HUNTERS

Caribou are perfectly adapted to the bleak, apparently inhospitable Barren Grounds of northern Labrador, and the Native peoples of that region were superbly adapted to hunting caribou. Even today, many of the Innu and Inuit in the towns along the Labrador coast still head inland on snowmobiles for the annual caribou hunt.

COMEDIANS

Maybe you have to be able to laugh to get along in Newfoundland. Maybe it's that Irish-Newfoundland gift for talk, honed for years around the stove in some outport kitchen. Or maybe it's just a product of the lively cultural and entertainment community in St. John's. But year after year, many of Canada's brightest, funniest, most successful comedians and satirists get their start in Newfoundland.

FAMOUS AND INFAMOUS

DAVID BLACKWOOD (1941-   )

The printmaker David Blackwood of Wesleyville, Newfoundland, has spent most of his life in Ontario, but his art is inspired by the island of his ancestors. A descendant of fishermen, sea captains, and sealers, he depicts the heroic old Newfoundland in his art.

CHARLOTTE BOWRING

Charlotte Price married a watchmaker, Ben Bowring, and immigrated to St. John's with him in 1816. While he practised his trade, she opened a shop. Soon the shop was doing better than the watchmaking trade. Charlotte's husband and their sons moved into the business and built up Bowrings, a leading St. John's retail outfit that is now known right across Canada.

JOHN CABOT (D. 1498)

He was born Giovanni Caboto, in Genoa, Italy. It was the English king and the merchant-sailors of Bristol, however, who sent John Cabot westwards in 1497 to see whether Christopher Columbus's discoveries could be matched farther north. They could. Cabot found "the new founde lande" and brought back news that you could catch fish by dropping a basket over the side of the ship. Sadly, Cabot went back to the new isle in 1498 and was never heard from again. But the rush to harvest the Grand Banks had begun.

PETER EASTON
(LATE SIXTEENTH-SEVENTEENTH CENTURY)

Who protected the fishermen? No one. In 1612, the pirate captain Peter Easton swooped in to take control of Harbour Grace. No one could stand up against his cannons and fighting men, and all summer long Easton helped himself to other people's ships, food, supplies. He wanted sailors, too. Some fishermen joined the pirate fleet and sailed away with him. When word got back that Captain Easton had plundered a golden galleon from Spain, people began to talk more fondly of the Pirate Admiral of Harbour Grace.

WILFRED GRENFELL (1865-1940)

In the 1890s, Wilfred Grenfell, an English doctor and missionary, travelled to Labrador, where he found thousands of transient fishing families and a few "livyers" (those who lived there year-round) who had almost no medical help and lived in great poverty. Grenfell devoted his life to them. He became famous as "Grenfell of Labrador" because of his fundraising work. He built hospitals, nursing stations, workshops, and an orphanage to serve the people of Labrador and northern Newfoundland.

PATRICK MORRIS (1789-1849)

Patrick Morris was an Irish Catholic who immigrated to St. John's in about 1804 and prospered as a merchant. But he did not forget the poor Irish immigrants to Newfoundland. He began campaigning for elected government. When an assembly was created, he used it to fight for the rights of Catholics and the needs of ordinary immigrants and fishing families. Newfoundland honours Patrick Morris as a champion of democracy.

SHAWNANDITHIT (ABOUT 1801-1829)

Newfoundlanders first realized that the Beothuk people of the island were dying fast in 1823, when a young Beothuk woman named Shawnandithit surrendered, starving, to fishers on the north coast. They called her Nancy April, for the month of her capture. She went to live in St. John's and told the explorer William Cormack about her people. Shawnandithit died of tuberculosis in 1829. When Cormack went to her home district, he found all the Beothuk places silent and abandoned. Shawnandithit had been the last of her people.

JOSEPH SMALLWOOD (1900-1991)

"I chose Canada" was Joey Smallwood's proudest boast and the title of his memoirs. He was a broadcaster and a failed pig farmer in 1946, when he decided that only by joining Canada could Newfoundlanders share in the prosperity of the modern world. Many proud Newfoundlanders accused him of selling out their country. But Joey, a brilliant speaker and a fearless campaigner, persuaded just enough people to follow his lead. He made Newfoundland the tenth province of Canada in 1949 and led it as premier until 1972.

Joseph Smallwood signs the document that admits the tenth province into Confederation.

LAW AND ORDER

The Confederation Building in St. John's.

Newfoundland and Labrador is the official name of the province. The name Newfoundland – and Terre-Neuve (French) and Tierra Neuva (Portuguese) – came into use soon after John Cabot's discovery. Labrador was named for a early Portuguese explorer, Joao Fernandes Lavrador.

The people of Newfoundland and Labrador elect a legislature of fifty-two men and women, called members of the Legislative Assembly (MLAs). The party leader who is supported by a majority of MLAs becomes premier and appoints a Cabinet of ministers to run the government. The Legislative Assembly meets in St. John's at the Confederation Building, Canada's newest provincial legislature (built in 1959) and the most modern in style. Newfoundland is represented in Ottawa by six senators and seven members of Parliament.

Newfoundland politics have always been lively and diverse. Rivalries between the outports and "town," and between Catholics and Protestants, have occasionally been fierce. Labradorians sometimes feel like a neglected minority.

One of the longest-running political disputes involves the Labrador boundary. As early as 1922, before Newfoundland even joined Canada, politicians argued about where the border between Labrador and Quebec lay, with Canada maintaining that Labrador could claim only a thin strip of coastline. In 1927, however, the courts confirmed that Labrador owned a much larger area, one that included all the land drained by Labrador's rivers. That remains the boundary between Quebec and Labrador, though the province of Quebec sometimes suggests that at least some of Labrador should belong to it.

NATIVES AND THEIR LAND CLAIMS

Though the Beothuk peoples of Newfoundland died out in the 1820s, several Native communities can still be found in Newfoundland and Labrador today. Mi'kmaq who migrated across from the mainland have a reserve at Conne River, on Newfoundland's south shore. The Labrador Inuit, or Labradormiut, traditionally lived all along the rugged seacoast of northern Labrador. Today most live in Makkovik, Nain, and other coastal villages. And the Innu live in several communities in inland Labrador and also on the coast. They maintain their traditional hunting ways across the interior of Labrador.

All three groups work to preserve their heritage and assert their land claims. The Innu believe that air force training flights across Labrador damage their caribou hunting, and the Labrador Inuit have been developing a substantial land claim in northern Labrador.

Moravian missionaries resettled most Labrador Inuit in the communities of Nain, Hopedale, and Makkovik.

JOINED CONFEDERATION:
March 31, 1949

PROVINCIAL MOTTO:
Quaerite prime regnum dei (Seek ye first the kingdom of God)

PROVINCIAL FLOWER:
Pitcher plant

AREA:
404,500 square kilometres

HIGHEST POINT:
Mount Caubvick, in the Torngat Mountains
(1,652 metres above sea level)

POPULATION:
521,930

GROWTH RATE:
Down by 7 per cent since 1996

CAPITAL:
St. John's

MAIN CITIES:
St. John's (172,918 in 2001), Corner Brook (25,747), Gander (11,254)

NEWFOUNDLAND GOVERNMENT INFORMATION ON THE INTERNET:
www.gov.nf.ca

Newfoundland's floral emblem, the pitcher plant, eats bugs! A pool of water and oil in its petals attracts insects, and the plant traps and digests them.

Newfoundland needs its own dictionary to list all the special words only Newfoundlanders use. It is said that when two fishers meet, all they will say is "Arn?" and "Narn!" They are talking about fish. *Arn* means "any," *narn* means "none."

angishore (n.)	a weak, miserable person
ballyrag (v.)	to abuse
bonna winkie (n.)	blind man's bluff
callibogus (n.)	a traditional Newfoundland drink made with spruce beer, molasses, and dark rum
dead-man's pinch (n.)	a small bruise that appears with out any apparent cause
dumbledore (n.)	a bumblebee
flahoolach (adj.)	lavish, extravagant
gowdy (adj.)	awkward
jinker (n.)	one who brings bad luck
loodle-laddle (n.)	a funny name given to an object in order to puzzle a child
mauzy (adj.)	misty
nish (adj.)	tender
puffing-pig (n.)	a porpoise
slob (n.)	newly frozen ice
switchel (n.)	cold tea
teeveen (n.)	a patch on a boat
tuckamore (n.)	a patch of trees

Nowhere in North America are place names so charming and unusual as in Newfoundland and Labrador. Newfoundland communities include Come by Chance, Ha Ha Bay, Joe Batt's Arm, and Calves Nose. You can visit Bad Bay, Bleak Island, Misery Point, and Cape Despair, but you can also go to Heart's Delight, Heart's Content, Heart's Desire, and Little Heart's Ease.

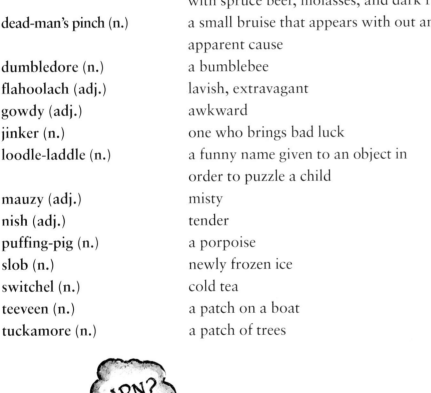

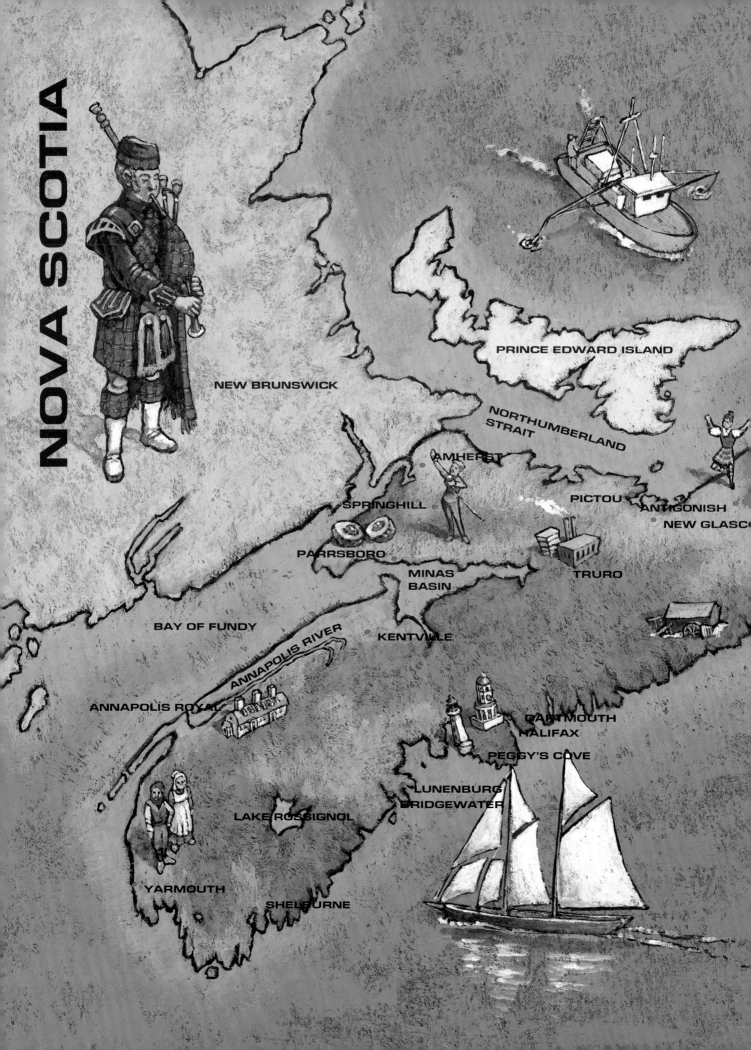

NOVA SCOTIA

NEW BRUNSWICK

PRINCE EDWARD ISLAND

NORTHUMBERLAND STRAIT

AMHERST

SPRINGHILL

PICTOU

ANTIGONISH

NEW GLASC

PARRSBORO

MINAS BASIN

TRURO

BAY OF FUNDY

KENTVILLE

ANNAPOLIS RIVER

ANNAPOLIS ROYAL

DARTMOUTH

HALIFAX

PEGGY'S COVE

LAKE ROSSIGNOL

LUNENBURG

BRIDGEWATER

YARMOUTH

SHELBURNE

ALMOST AN ISLAND

Almost an island, Nova Scotia is at no point more than 130 kilometres from salt water; only a narrow isthmus joins the province to the North American mainland. Nova Scotia has thirty-nine hundred islands, and one of them, Cape Breton Island, makes up 20 per cent of the province.

Nova Scotia ("New Scotland" in Latin) got its name from early Scots colonists, but most of the original settlers who joined its Mi'kmaq people were French who called themselves Acadians. Britain took over the French colony, Acadia, in 1710, and British settlement really began when Halifax was founded in 1749. Brutal wars confirmed that Nova Scotia would remain British, and for a while, all of what is now the Maritimes was part of Nova Scotia. Prince Edward Island and New Brunswick later became separate colonies, and Cape Breton Island was separate for a time too.

When it settled into its current borders, Nova Scotia remained the largest and most influential Atlantic colony. Nova Scotians remember that Canada's earliest universities, its first writers, its early business dynasties, and many of its great thinkers have come from their province. Nova Scotian trading ships roamed the world's oceans; its fishing schooners prospered.

Nova Scotia still has the largest population of the four Atlantic provinces, and Halifax is the largest city in the region. The Scottish connection is preserved in the large Scots populations of northeastern Nova Scotia and Cape Breton Island, but Nova Scotia's ethnic mix also includes Irish, English, Acadian, Loyalist American, German, and a growing number of immigrant communities.

CAPE BRETON ISLAND

SYDNEY MINES

GLACE BAY

SYDNEY

LOUISBOURG

BRAS D'OR LAKE

STRAIT OF CANSO

CHEDABUCTO BAY

CANSO

ATLANTIC OCEAN

SABLE ISLAND

Nova Scotia rests on the rock of the Atlantic Uplands, the remains of an ancient mountain range that is now ground down and broken into several sections. One section forms most of the southwestern peninsula. Another lies beneath the isthmus linking the province to New Brunswick. Yet another shapes the rugged highlands of Cape Breton Island. Most of the province is hilly, rocky country.

ANNAPOLIS BASIN AND VALLEY

Only a tenth of Nova Scotia makes good farmland. Much of the best of that lies in the gentle valley of the Annapolis River. In the 1650s, French settlers began to build dikes along the tidal marshes of the bay and the river. Sheltered from the sea, the old marshes became rich farmland. Today farms and orchards continue to thrive in what Nova Scotians know as "the Valley."

THE COASTAL HARBOURS

"One of the finest harbours in the world!" Sailors from Europe said that about dozens of sheltered bays and inlets when they first explored the twisted granite coast of Nova Scotia. Whole fleets could anchor in Chebucto Bay, and as a result, Halifax became the province's great seaport and its capital. But much of Nova Scotia's early prosperity was built by sailors and shipbuilders in scores of smaller communities along the coast.

CAPE BRETON HIGHLANDS

Ancient rock, thrust up to form a high plateau, scoured by ice and cut by rivers that drop steeply to the surrounding ocean: in less than a thousand square kilometres, the highlands of Cape Breton offer some of Canada's

The lush, gentle farmland of the Annapolis Valley.

most spectacular landscapes. Moose, bobcat, lynx, and bear still roam the area, which has been a national park since 1936.

SABLE ISLAND

Like Newfoundland, Nova Scotia has its own shallow-water "banks" rich in marine life. Three hundred kilometres out from Halifax, these shallows rise to form a sandbank called Sable Island. For five hundred years, Sable Island has been both feared as a risk to ships and admired for its wild beauty. Its best-known residents are the herds of wild horses that have made the island home for hundreds of years.

Driving the Cabot Trail on Cape Breton Island.

1867   Nova Scotia prided itself on being one of Britain's oldest, most prosperous colonies, and many Nova Scotians did not want to become junior partners in the new nation called Canada. After fierce debate, Nova Scotia's elected legislators voted in favour of Confederation, but many ordinary Nova Scotians disapproved. Soon after Confederation was completed, they threw most of the pro-Confederation politicians out of office.

1886   William S. Fielding was re-elected premier on his promise to take Nova Scotia out of Confederation. With the province's debts growing and its sailing fleet in steady decline, many Nova Scotians wondered if joining Canada had been a mistake. But to others, coal, iron, and railways gave hope.

Premier William S. Fielding.

1905   Canada's largest and most efficient steel plant opened at Sydney Mines, on Cape Breton Island. Canada's first steel mill had opened at Pictou in the 1880s.

1917   On December 6, two ships collided in the narrows at the entrance to Halifax Harbour, which was crowded with naval vessels and cargo ships. One, the *Mont Blanc*, was loaded with explosives. It blew up, causing the greatest explosion ever made by humans up to that time. Much of the industrial North End was wiped out, and more than sixteen hundred people were killed.

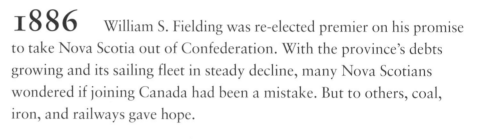

1921   Canada's most famous ship, the schooner *Bluenose*, was launched at Lunenburg. Under the command of Capt. Angus Walters, the *Bluenose* won almost every schooner race for twenty years – and brought in record fish catches too.

1930   Father Moses Coady helped found the United Maritime Fishermen's Co-operative, which worked to improve prices and trade conditions for hard-pressed Nova Scotian fishing families. The "co-op" movement soon became a powerful force, helping many disadvantaged communities improve their situation.

1941   The writer Hugh MacLennan published *Barometer Rising*, a novel set in Halifax during the explosion of 1917. MacLennan went on to become one of the leaders of the great expansion of Canadian writing in the following decades.

1955   Nova Scotia proudly opened the Canso Causeway, which carries the Trans-Canada Highway across Strait of Canso and joins Cape Breton Island to the Nova Scotia mainland. New highways and industries were part of the province's efforts to share in the wealth of the 1950s and catch up to the richer provinces of central Canada.

1956   A mine disaster at Springhill killed thirty-nine miners. Two years later, a second one killed seventy-four miners.

1970   The oil tanker *Arrow* sank in Chedabucto Bay, threatening the fishing industry and polluting the rich waters and beautiful shores. Just a year later, exploration companies struck natural gas near Sable Island, launching Nova Scotia's own oil-and-gas industry.

1998   The Liberal government called a provincial election, and the voters produced a three-way tie, with the Liberals, the New Democrats, and the Conservatives winning almost the same number of seats. When another election was held the next year, many observers thought there might be another tie – or possibly the first New Democratic government in the province. Instead, the Conservatives, led by John Hamm, won a majority.

MI'KMAQ

When the first French colonizers came to Nova Scotia in 1604, they received a hospitable welcome from the Mi'kmaq peoples, who had already been trading with travelling fishermen for most of a century. The Mi'kmaq were hunters and gatherers who followed a seasonal round that took them to much of Nova Scotia. Today about twenty thousand Mi'kmaq maintain several reserves in the province, and they continue to defend their treaty rights and land claims.

ACADIANS

When a few families came from France to Nova Scotia about 1650, they saw that the best land lay on the tidal flats along the Bay of Fundy. They built dikes to keep out the Fundy tides, then raised their crops and animals on fertile flatlands recovered from the sea.

While France and England fought over Nova Scotia for a century, the French settlers, who called themselves Acadians, mostly tried to stay out of the conflict. But they could not. With another war looming in 1755, the British rounded up all the Acadians they could find and shipped them away. Some escaped, and a few later returned. Today most Acadians live in New Brunswick, but there are still Acadian populations in southwestern Nova Scotia, on Cape Breton Island, and in PEI.

An eighteenth-century view of Annapolis Royal.

SOUTH SHORE GERMANS

When Britain wanted to populate Nova Scotia with loyal settlers in the 1750s, some of the immigrants it brought in were actually Germans (because King George II of Britain was also a German prince). Many of the German immigrants settled the South Shore, around Lunenburg. There is still a strong German flavour in that region, as well as many distinctive German-influenced names.

PLANTERS

Across the Maritime provinces, many families speak proudly of a Loyalist ancestor who settled in Nova Scotia or New Brunswick in 1783 or 1784. (The Loyalists sided with Britain during the American Revolution.) The Planters, however, came even earlier. These New Englanders settled Nova Scotia and New Brunswick around 1760, often on lands originally cleared by the then exiled Acadians. They took their name from an old word for those who "planted" new settlements.

HIGHLAND SCOTS

In the Highlands of Scotland in the early 1800s, landlords found raising sheep more profitable than renting land to poor farm families. They turned the families out of their homes, and many of these so-called Highland Scots began to pour into Canada. Whole districts of mainland Nova Scotia and Cape Breton were peopled by Gaelic-speaking Highland families driven out by what came to be called the Clearances. Today Cape Breton Island is still home to Canada's largest and liveliest Gaelic-speaking community, and Scots influences remain strong throughout eastern Nova Scotia.

Nova Scotia is almost the only place in North America where Gaelic is spoken.

AFRICAN NOVA SCOTIANS

Nova Scotia's black community is old and deep-rooted. As many as a third of the Loyalist immigrants who came to Nova Scotia in 1783 were blacks. Many of them, disgusted by the discrimination they faced, moved on to Sierra Leone in Africa a few years later. But the black Nova Scotian community endured.

In the 1960s, urban renewal in Halifax destroyed the black neighbourhood called Africville, causing fierce protest and the strengthening of black community organizations.

A black woodcutter at Shelburne, 1788.

BLUEBERRY GRUNT

Some Nova Scotians say the great Nova Scotia meal is Solomon Grundy, a marinated herring dish. You may prefer blueberry grunt, which Nova Scotians make from their delicious wild blueberries.

1 pint (500ml) blueberries
1/2 cup (125 mL) sugar
1 cup (250 mL) water
1 1/2 cup (375 mL) flour
2 tsp (10 mL) baking powder
2 tsp (10 mL) grated orange rind
1/4 tsp (1 mL) nutmeg

1/4 tsp (1 mL) salt
3/4 cup (175 mL) milk

Simmer berries, sugar, and water until thick and just beginning to bubble. Lower heat. In a bowl, mix flour, baking powder, orange rind, and seasonings, and stir in milk to moisten. Drop batter by spoonfuls into blueberry mix. Cover and cook 15 minutes or until dumplings puff up. Serve remaining sauce over dumplings while hot.

HALIFAX

Halifax was founded as a seaport and protected by a citadel. One of the bastions of the British Empire, it was called the Warden of the North, and evidence of its history is everywhere. Halifax is still the Atlantic headquarters of the Canadian navy. It is also a lively modern city, a centre of politics, trade, culture, and intellectual life for all of eastern Canada.

Survivors of the devastating Springhill mine disaster.

INDUSTRIAL CAPE BRETON

Say the words "Cape Breton" and many Canadians will think of spectacular scenery. But the Sydney–Glace Bay–Sydney Mines area has long been an industrial powerhouse, with coal mines, steel mills, and related industries all around. In this region, Scots-Gaelic culture and working-class culture mix together. At the Glace Bay Miners Museum, visitors learn about the dangerous working conditions faced by Cape Breton coal miners – and the tight-knit communities they built to sustain themselves. Sydney struggles to maintain its industrial traditions and to clean up some of the environmental problems created by unsafe practices in the past.

ANNAPOLIS ROYAL

Samuel de Champlain was among the founders of Port-Royal, which grew into the leading town of French Acadia. Renamed Annapolis Royal in honour of Britain's Queen Anne, the town is today a charming heritage community with attractive bed-and-breakfasts, antique shops, and restaurants. Just down the road, Champlain's original habitation has been reconstructed as a historic site. Along the Annapolis River, engineers continue to experiment with ways to generate hydroelectric power from the surging tides.

YARMOUTH

A hundred years ago, Saint John, New Brunswick, was the only place in Canada that was home port to more shipping tonnage than Yarmouth. This small town's sailing ships, most of them built nearby, were hauling freight to ports from Shanghai to New York. Yarmouth is quieter today, but it remains the commercial centre of southeastern Nova Scotia, and the handsome homes built by the town's merchants and shipowners still command the hills about the harbour.

LOUISBOURG

In the early 1700s, Louisbourg was the busiest place in Maritime Canada, a fortified town and seaport that was the centre of French trade and military power on the Atlantic coast. The British built Halifax to rival it, and then they captured and abandoned Louisbourg in 1758. Today part of the eighteenth-century city has risen again at Fortress of Louisbourg National Historic Park, one of the world's great historic recreations. It attracts many thousands of visitors annually.

The Fortress of Louisbourg.

Canada's most famous schooner, the Bluenose, *under full sail, 1921.*

SCHOONER SAILORS

"Wooden ships with iron men," they called the Nova Scotia shipping fleet in the mid-1800s. Nearly every local harbour became a shipbuilding centre, and trim Nova Scotian sailing ships were soon found roving the world's oceans. But the sailors were really flesh and blood, not iron. It was a tough, dangerous line of work, and the Bluenoses, as Nova Scotians are sometimes called, were among the best in the world at it.

COAL MINERS

They started digging coal out of the cliffs near Glace Bay early in the 1700s, and coal has been part of the Nova Scotia economy ever since. But terrible accidents have also long been part of coal mining. Seventy-four men died, three kilometres down, in the Springhill mine disaster of 1958. Today most coal is mined in open pits, with less risk to miners' lives. But in 1992, an explosion deep inside the Westray mine, in Pictou County, killed twenty-six miners.

FOLK MUSICIANS

Music has been part of the Nova Scotian heritage for centuries. Anne Murray emerged from Springhill to become an international singing star in the 1970s, and in the 1990s, many East Coast musicians gained worldwide attention. The Celtic folk-music family the Rankins, the balladeer Rita MacNeil, the fiddlers Ashley MacIsaac and Natalie McMaster, and the pop-rockers Sloan are just a few of the internationally successful top acts that have remained rooted in Atlantic Canada and its musical styles.

GEMSTONE HUNTERS

Watch those rocks! Around Parrsboro, gem hunters split open plain round rocks called geodes, hoping to find beautifully coloured quartz crystals gleaming inside the hollow core. The chance of finding a spectacular geode has made the Bay of Fundy shore a favourite spot of collectors, and several "rock shops" and galleries welcome them.

CRAFTSPEOPLE

Every province has distinctive crafts. Nova Scotia, with its long-established traditions and thriving tourist industry, has a particularly well-developed craft industry. Small workshops and larger galleries around the province feature the work of many local artisans, including woodworkers, potters, weavers, and silversmiths. There is even a small distillery making Scotch whisky.

UNIVERSITY PROFESSORS

Nova Scotia was an early centre of learning in Canada. King's College in Halifax, the first university in Canada (founded 1789), is one of nine universities in the province. Many are small schools, located in smaller centres such as Wolfville, Church Point, and Antigonish, but several draw students from all over Canada.

HELEN CREIGHTON (1899-1989)

When Helen Creighton started to collect the folk songs and stories of Nova Scotia, tape recorders were so large and heavy that she pushed hers along in a wheelbarrow. Thanks to her efforts, the folklore of old Nova Scotia villages, farms, and workplaces has been preserved.

WILLIAM S. FIELDING (1848-1929)

When he had been premier for two years, William Fielding declared that Nova Scotia would be better off on its own, and he won re-election promising to take his province out of Confederation. But soon after, Nova Scotians rejected the anti-confederates in a federal election. Fielding decided there was no real support for separation, and the whole idea died.

THOMAS CHANDLER HALIBURTON (1796-1865)

Tom Haliburton prospered as a lawyer and a judge, but he is better remembered as a writer – indeed as the first internationally famous Canadian writer. He wrote serious histories and political pamphlets, but his best-known book was his funniest: *The Clockmaker*, with its hero, Sam Slick of Slickville, a wise-cracking Yankee.

Joseph Howe, thinker and politician, around 1871.

JOSEPH HOWE (1804-1873)

It was done "without a blow struck or a pane of glass broken," said Joseph Howe proudly. In February 1848, a government answerable to the voters' elected representatives took power in Halifax, making Nova Scotia the first self-governing colony anywhere in the British Empire. Howe, the architect of the achievement, was one of Canada's greatest political thinkers. In 1864, he would oppose Confederation because he considered the terms unfair to his beloved Nova Scotia.

ISAAC WALTON KILLAM (1885-1955)

Born in Yarmouth, Isaac Killam began life as a bank clerk and prospered as a financier. By the 1920s, he was said to be Canada's richest (and most secretive) millionaire. He lived much of his life in Montreal, but he left a fortune in donations to Nova Scotia, where the Halifax children's hospital is named for him.

ANNA LEONOWENS (1834-1915)

Anna Leonowens went to Siam (now Thailand) and became governess to the sixty-seven children in King Mongkut's royal household. The book she wrote about her life as "Mem Cha" (Madame dear) became world famous and inspired the musical *The King and I*. When her daughter married a Halifax banker, Leonowens moved there. She became a feminist writer and lecturer, and also helped found the Nova Scotia College of Art and Design.

DONALD "JUNIOR" MARSHALL (1953-   )

In 1971, after his buddy was killed in a fight in Sydney, sixteen-year-old Junior Marshall was arrested, tried, and convicted for murder. But he always swore he was innocent, and in 1983, after spending eleven years in jail for a crime he did not commit, he was freed. Later he helped his Mi'kmaq people claim their rights to fish and hunt, and in 1999 "the Marshall case" became an important landmark for Native rights.

Wrongly convicted Donald Marshall, free at last.

J. B. MCLACHLAN (1869-1937)

In industrial Cape Breton, miners and steelworkers struggled hard against powerful companies and unsympathetic governments. Their fiery leader was James McLachlan, who built up the United Mine Workers in Nova Scotia, led many strikes, and was frequently sent to jail. He ran for political office as a socialist and a Communist, but his lifelong motto came from the Bible: "Plead the cause of the poor and needy."

FATHER JIMMY TOMPKINS (1870-1953)

Father Jimmy Tompkins, a Catholic priest and teacher, wanted his university to do more to help the working people of eastern Nova Scotia. Instead, his bishop sent him as parish priest to the poor fishermen of remote Canso Island. Father Jimmy helped them organize credit unions, marketing co-ops, labour unions, and schools for adults. Then he moved on to Reserve Mines, on Cape Breton Island, where he continued to teach self-help and self-reliance for working people. The campaign Father Jimmy inspired became the Antigonish Movement, and today it helps ordinary Nova Scotians – and less fortunate people around the world – improve their lives through education and organization.

LAW AND ORDER

Province House in Halifax.

Nova Scotia, Latin for "New Scotland," got that name in 1629, when Sir William Alexander decided to found a colony north of New England.

Nova Scotia's government is led by a premier and his Cabinet, which is appointed by the provincial lieutenant-governor but answerable to the fifty-two elected members of the House of Assembly. The legislature meets at Province House in Halifax, a handsome Georgian building designed by John Merrick and built in 1811–19. It is the oldest provincial legislature in Canada. Until 1928, Nova Scotia also had an upper house, the Legislative Council.

Nova Scotians elect eleven members to the Canadian House of Commons in Ottawa, and there are ten appointed senators. Nova Scotian women campaigned vigorously for the vote in the late 1800s, and they finally won the right in 1920.

Once Nova Scotians settle on a premier, they tend to stick with him.

Did you know that Nova Scotia's boundaries once included both New Brunswick and Prince Edward Island? On the other hand, Cape Breton Island was a separate colony as recently as the early 1800s.

Angus L. Macdonald was premier for seven years in the 1930s, went away to Ottawa for five years, then came back to be premier for nine more years. George Henry Murray was premier for twenty-six years (from 1896 to 1923), which is still a record in Canada. He is not remembered for much else.

Three Nova Scotians have been prime minister. Sir John Thompson (1892–94) died in office, and Sir Charles Tupper (1896) was defeated by Wilfrid Laurier soon after taking power. But Sir Robert Borden was Canada's leader from 1911 to 1920, years that included the First World War.

MARITIME UNION

In 1864, Nova Scotia, New Brunswick, and Prince Edward Island were meeting to discuss uniting together when the idea of a federation of all the British colonies in North America took over. Even though Confederation did indeed go ahead, these three provinces have continued to debate the merits of Maritime Union over the years.

Supporters of Maritime Union argue that if the three provinces united, they could work more effectively to pursue the region's goals. Also, they would have one government to pay for instead of three.

But doubts and questions always arise. What would the new province be called? Where would the capital be? Nova Scotians sometimes assume that their province, the largest and oldest of the three, would take the lead in any union – an assumption that cools the enthusiasm of the other two!

Sir Charles Tupper, Nova Scotia's premier and briefly prime minister of Canada.

Yet despite all the talk over many years, Maritime Union has never seemed very close. Today the three provinces co-operate in the Atlantic Provinces Economic Council and other organizations intended to help the whole region. But Maritime Union seems not much more likely now than it did in 1867.

JOINED CONFEDERATION:
July 1, 1867

PROVINCIAL MOTTO:
Munit haec et altera vincit (One defends and the other conquers)

PROVINCIAL FLOWER:
Mayflower

AREA:
55,491 square kilometres

HIGHEST POINT:
Cape Breton Highlands (532 metres above sea level)

POPULATION:
908,002

GROWTH RATE:
Down by 0.1 per cent since 1996

CAPITAL:
Halifax

MAIN CITIES:
Halifax-Dartmouth (359,111 in 2001), Sydney (105,968)

**NOVA SCOTIA GOVERNMENT INFORMATION
ON THE INTERNET:**
www.gov.ns.ca

THE NOVA SCOTIA SONG

It's a strange thing that Nova Scotia's favourite song is about going away from the island. But sometimes sad songs are the best songs. "The Nova Scotia Song," sometimes more popularly called "Farewell to Nova Scotia," is the lament of a poor sailor obliged to set sail once more. Uncovered and published by the folklorist Helen Creighton, it's practically the provincial anthem.

1.
The sun was setting in the west,
The birds were singing in
    every tree,
All nature seemed inclined
    for rest,
But still there was no rest for me.

Chorus:
Farewell to Nova Scotia, the
    sea-bound coast!
Let your mountains dark
    and dreary be,
For when I am far away on
    the briny ocean tossed
Will you ever heave a sigh and
    a wish for me?

2.
I grieve to leave my native land,
I grieve to leave my comrades all,
And my parents whom I hold
    so dear,
And the bonny, bonny lass that
    I do adore.

Chorus

3.
The drums they do beat and the
    wars do alarm.
The captain calls, we must obey,
So farewell, farewell to Nova
    Scotia's charms,
For it's early in the morning I am
    far, far away.

Chorus

4.
I have three brothers and they
    are at rest,
Their arms are folded on
    their breast,
But a poor simple sailor just
    like me
Must be tossed and driven on
    the dark blue sea.

Chorus

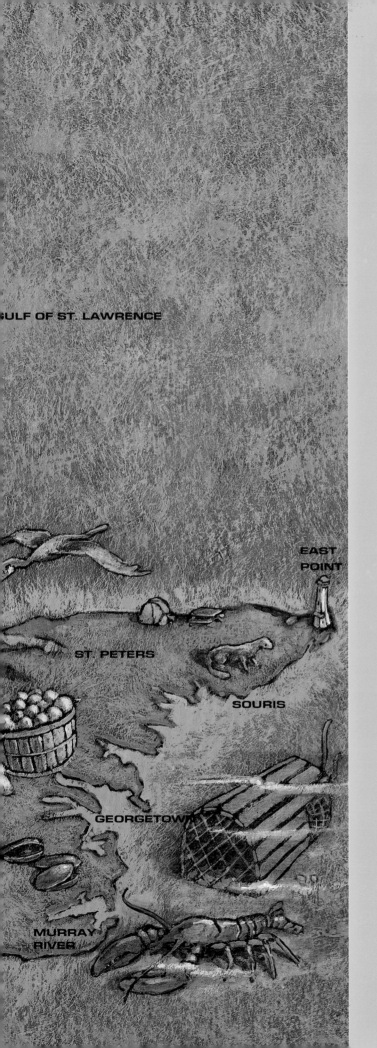

GULF OF ST. LAWRENCE

EAST
POINT

ST. PETERS

SOURIS

GEORGETOWN

MURRAY
RIVER

THE GARDEN IN THE GULF

In 1534, the explorer Jacques Cartier called Prince Edward Island "the fairest land that may possibly be seen." Three hundred and thirty years later, a Father of Confederation, George Brown, arrived from Toronto and called it "as pretty a country as you ever put your eye on." Millions of visitors to Canada's smallest province agree with both of them.

There are fewer city-dwellers in Prince Edward Island than in any other province. Yet the Island is Canada's most densely populated province, with twenty-three people for every square kilometre. Farming and fishing can be difficult ways to earn a living, and Prince Edward Island is a relatively poor province, in need of development and investment. Beneath its beauty, charm, and history, the Island strives to share in Canada's prosperity without losing its distinct culture and style.

Island pride and the Islanders' independent way of life are always important issues in the province. In the 1980s, Islanders debated whether to permit a bridge to the mainland. The debate brought out their traditional struggle to balance progress with protection for the Island's special character. In a province-wide referendum, voters narrowly approved the "fixed link," and the thirteen-kilometre Confederation Bridge opened in 1997.

About five thousand years ago, the rising waters of the Gulf of St. Lawrence cut Prince Edward Island from the mainland. It has been affectionately called "a patch of sandbank in the gulf." Indeed, the entire Island is built on sand and gravel that was laid down in the gulf long ago and slowly crushed into sandstone and sedimentary rock. The landscapes of the Island vary from rugged cliffs and dunes along the shore to sheltered harbours behind the outer coast and gently rolling fields and woodlots inland.

NORTH COAST SAND DUNES

The north coast is a fragile seascape. Its cliffs are constantly being eroded by the surf, and its dunes and sandbars shift with the seasons. Today's lighthouse at East Point stands hundreds of metres from the site of the original light, which is now out in the ocean. Behind the dunes and sandbanks, the salt marshes and bays support shellfish, seabirds, and small animals, such as muskrats, minks, and foxes.

THE HILLSBOROUGH RIVER

Prince Edward Island has few true rivers, but Islanders use the name to describe the long saltwater inlets that cut deep into their land. One of them, the Hillsborough River, flows into the Northumberland Strait just east of Charlottetown. On its banks is Scotchfort, one of two Mi'kmaq communities of Prince Edward Island.

The Island's unique red soil makes for fertile farmland.

RED SOIL FARMLAND

The gentle climate and rich red soils have made Prince Edward Island "the garden of the gulf." The striking red colour of the soil comes from iron oxides in the ground. The largest crop Island farmers produce is potatoes, of which they grow more than 600,000 tonnes a year. Some go in frozen french fry packages. The Island also ships high-quality seed potatoes all over the world.

MURRAY RIVER

What are those long rows of dots tracing a grid pattern across the placid surface of the sheltered inlet at Murray River? They are the buoys that support dangling lines where succulent blue mussels are "farmed." The mussels grow on these underwater lines and can be hauled up when they are large enough to harvest.

Islanders have long drawn a living from the sea. Mussels, oysters, scallops, and lobsters are just as important as fish among PEI "crops." Sheltered inlets like Murray River, St. Peters Bay, and Malpeque Bay are rich marine ecosystems where seals and cormorants are as common as mussel farmers.

The soil of Prince Edward Island is red because it contains iron oxide – and it is rusting.

MOMENTS

The Fathers of Confederation at Charlottetown, 1864.

1864 Charlottetown hosted the political conference that launched Canada's Confederation. But Islanders decided they did not like the "deal" they were offered and chose not to become Canadians – and they stayed out for several years.

1873 Canada improved its "terms of union," and Prince Edward Island became the seventh province. When the governor general came to visit, he declared that Islanders were "quite under the impression that it is the Dominion that has been annexed to Prince Edward Island."

1880 In the 1880s, Prince Edward Island boasted one of the world's great shipping fleets. Its ships and schooners carried freight around the world's oceans, and every Island harbour was also a shipyard. But the day of wind-powered wooden ships was ending, and the Island's fleet would swiftly fade away in the days of iron steamships.

1891 Migration out of Prince Edward Island meant that the province's population would decline for a time and then grow only very slowly in future decades. Prince Edward Island had nearly as many people in 1891 as it would have in 1961. For those who remained, Charles Dalton and Robert Oulton of Alberton promoted a new and valuable crop: silver foxes. Their pelts became furs for fashionable ladies in faraway cities.

1908 Islanders have generally wanted to protect their traditional Island ways of life. In 1908, they decided that one way to do that was to ban automobiles. That decision did not last long.

1921 Prince Edward Island suffered from the highest tuberculosis rate of any province. A Red Cross nurse, Amy McMahon, launched an Island-wide public health campaign to promote hygiene, sanitation, and healthy diets. In later years, Dr. W. J. P. Kennedy continued the fight against the disease.

1931   The Great Depression brought hard times to many islanders, but their charitable impulses remained strong. They sent sixty boxcars of relief supplies to the drought-stricken farmers of Saskatchewan.

1939   Almost half of the Island's men volunteered for the armed forces in the Second World War, one of the highest rates anywhere in Canada. Island-born Bill Reid, who started his career with the Prince Edward Island Highlanders, served in the Canadian army's Italian campaign, received several wounds and several medals, and became a general.

1951   Nine out of ten Island farms still depended on horses (there were twenty-one thousand of them), and the average Island kid walked to a one-room school just down the road. But the day of tractors, automobiles, paved roads, and school buses was coming fast. The isolation of small communities faded, but once Islanders could drive their new cars on the new roads into town, many country stores, schools, and churches began to close down.

1964   On the hundredth anniversary of the Charlottetown Conference, the Confederation Centre for the Arts opened in the provincial capital. The great hit of its theatre festival was the long-running musical *Anne of Green Gables*.

1997   After furious debate, Islanders opened "the fixed link." For the first time, a bridge – from Borden, Prince Edward Island, to Cape Tormentine, New Brunswick – joined the Island and the mainland. The all-weather, all-season crossing is named the Confederation Bridge.

PEOPLES

A Mi'kmaq family makes its winter hunting rounds.

MI'KMAQ

The Mi'kmaq of the Maritimes always made the Island part of their seasonal rounds, often gathering shellfish along the northern shores. Today the PEI Mi'kmaq maintain two reserve communities, at Lennox Island and Scotchfort.

ENGLISH

Islanders are more British in origin than people in any other province. Many "ordinary" English families came to farm or fish on the Island. Meanwhile, middle-class Anglican immigrants from England dominated the government and "high society" for generations.

SCOTS

Ever since John MacDonald of Glenaladale led Highland Catholic settlers to Prince Edward Island in 1772, Scots Gaelic and Catholic culture

has been strongly present. Many Protestant Scots, often members of the Presbyterian Church, also immigrated to Prince Edward Island.

IRISH

Both Irish Protestants and Irish Catholics came to the Island early in the 1800s. By the late 1800s, Irish Catholics were a strong, vocal minority in Island politics and Island life. In 1945, James McGuigan from Hunter River, who was the archbishop of Toronto, became the first English-Canadian cardinal of the Roman Catholic Church.

ACADIANS

Acadian farm families began to migrate from the mainland to Ile St-Jean (as they called Prince Edward Island) in the 1720s. More sought refuge there from British troops in the 1750s. Many Island Acadians were deported in 1758, but some managed to return in later years. Today the Acadians are nearly 10 per cent of the Island population. Most Acadians live on the western end of the Island, facing New Brunswick's Acadian shore.

ELEGANT BAKED POTATOES

The Prince Edward Island Potato Board calls this a stylish way to serve PEI potatoes — crisp on the outside, lots of flavour on the inside.

4 PEI potatoes
2 tbsp (30 mL) melted butter
salt
1 tbsp (15 mL) chopped fresh parsley or thyme
    OR 1 tsp (5 mL) dried parsley or thyme
1/4 cup (50 mL) grated Cheddar cheese
2 tbsp (30 mL) grated Parmesan cheese

Scrub potatoes. Cut, crosswise, into thin slices, placing the handle of a wooden spoon beside the potato to prevent the knife from cutting all the way through.
Put potatoes in a baking dish, fan slightly, and drizzle with butter. Sprinkle with salt and herbs. Bake at 425°F (220°C) for 50 minutes. Remove from oven, sprinkle with cheeses. Bake 10 to 15 minutes longer, or until lightly browned and cheeses are melted. Makes four servings.

Prince Edward Island is one of the best-known Canadian places in Japan – because of the popularity of *Anne of Green Gables* there. Many Japanese visit Green Gables every year.

CHARLOTTETOWN

"The capital called Charlottetown is proposed to be built on the harbour of Port Joy between the York and Hillsborough Rivers, as being one of the best and nearly central parts of the Island," wrote the surveyor Samuel Holland in 1765. Charlottetown has thrived ever since. Although it has only sixty thousand people, it is the Island's largest city by far. As well as being the centre of business and government, Charlottetown is "downtown" to the rural population of much of the Island. Its historic sites and cultural centres draw many visitors every summer.

Every summer, Charlottetown's historic Victoria Row draws thousands of visitors and Islanders alike.

SUMMERSIDE

Only six kilometres of land separate the Northumberland Strait from the Gulf of St. Lawrence at Summerside, the island's second-largest city and the centre of Prince County. Many young Canadians have learned to fly at the nearby air force base.

GREEN GABLES

An imaginary farmhouse is one of the best-loved places on the Island. Lucy Maud Montgomery created Green Gables as the home of Matthew and Marilla Cuthbert, who take in the sprightly orphan girl

Anne Shirley. The house on which Green Gables was based attracts thousands of visitors every year to Cavendish, on the north shore.

CONFEDERATION BRIDGE

There are longer bridges in the world, but none that must face the powerful ice that builds up in the Northumberland Strait every winter. The bridge fulfils an old promise. In 1873, when the Island joined Confederation, Canada vowed to maintain "continuous communication" with the mainland. For the next century, ferry services maintained the link, but they were often interrupted by storms or ice. Since June 1, 1997, drivers have been able to cross the strait in ten minutes.

MISCOUCHE

The area from Miscouche to Abram-Village and over to Grand-Digue is the Région Evangeline, the Acadian corner of Prince Edward Island. Arsenaults and Gallants and other Acadian families have been farming and fishing this part of the Island – and also the north coast, near Rustico – for 250 years. The Musée Acadien in Miscouche preserves family records of Island Acadians.

The Confederation Bridge.

Harvesting Irish moss on horseback – still the most efficient means.

IRISH MOSS HARVESTERS

Wagons and horses working in the surf off Miminegash or another harbour of western Prince Edward Island mean the harvest of Irish moss is under way again. Irish moss is an algae; an extract called carageenin is a foaming and binding agent used in beer, cosmetics, ice cream, and many other commercial products. This part of Prince Edward Island produces half the world's supply of Canada's most valuable seaweed crop, and no one has developed a machine that does the job more efficiently than the horses and wagons.

TOURIST SERVICE WORKERS

Every year, Prince Edward Island attracts about eight visitors for every Islander. Tourism is almost as important to the local economy as farming or fishing. From Green Gables and Province House to campgrounds and deep-sea fishing tours, tourism touches every part of the Island.

SCALLOP PLANT WORKERS

Most Islanders fish close in to the shore, using small boats that make short trips before returning to local harbours. As a result, many local harbours on the Island have small, specialized fish plants to can, freeze, or preserve lobsters, scallops, or whatever catch the local boats pursue. Lobsters are the most valuable seafood product of Prince Edward Island.

VETERINARIANS

The Atlantic provinces have many farmers, but all their veterinarians were trained elsewhere until 1983, when the Atlantic Provinces Veterinary College opened in Charlottetown. The college serves all four Atlantic provinces. It teaches aquaculture veterinary sciences, as well as the care of traditional farm animals and household pets.

VETERANS AFFAIRS WORKERS

If you are seeking information about what your grandfather did in Canada's wars, Charlottetown may be the place to find it. Canada's Department of Veterans Affairs has offices in Prince Edward Island that honour and record the service of Canadian veterans.

A century ago, lobsters were often considered a poor people's food in Prince Edward Island. "We were so poor we had to eat lobsters we caught ourselves," people remembered.

FAMOUS AND INFAMOUS

Island poet Milton Acorn, 1970.

MILTON ACORN (1923-1986)

His fellow poets called Milton Acorn "the people's poet." He was the Island's poet too, a rough-and-tumble working man who wove images of Prince Edward Island into many of his finest poems.

JOSEPH-OCTAVE ARSENAULT (1828-1897)

In 1884, Joseph-Octave Arsenault organized the first Acadian congress on the Island. The Acadian community of western Prince Edward Island began to make its presence felt, and Arsenault became the first, and only, Acadian named to the Canadian Senate.

CATHERINE CALLBECK (1939-)

After running a family business and serving in both federal and provincial politics, Catherine Callbeck succeeded Joe Ghiz as premier of Prince Edward Island in 1993. One other woman (Rita Johnston of B.C.) had briefly headed a provincial government, but Callbeck became the first woman to fight and win a provincial election anywhere in Canada. She retired from politics and the premier's office in 1996.

STOMPIN' TOM CONNORS (1936-)

Born in New Brunswick but raised by adoptive parents in Skinners Pond, PEI, Tom Connors roamed Canada in his youth and began a singing career in Timmins, Ontario. He sang country songs about the people and places he encountered, accompanying himself on guitar and with his heel pounding down on his plywood "stomping board." In his most famous song, Stompin' Tom sang about "Bud the Spud" and the delicious potatoes from Prince Edward Island.

JOE GHIZ (1945-1996)

Joe Ghiz, the Charlottetown-born son of immigrant Syrian shopkeepers, went to Harvard University, became a lawyer, and was elected premier of the province in 1986. He was an important part of Canada's constitutional talks and a proud spokesperson for multiculturalism.

ROBERT HARRIS (1849-1919) AND WILLIAM CRITCHLOW HARRIS (1854-1913)

Robert, one of Canada's finest portrait painters, painted *The Fathers of Confederation* in 1884. He worked in Montreal much of his life, but his

58

Meeting of the School Trustees captured the one-room schools of his Island home. Meanwhile, his younger brother, William, stayed home, became an architect, and designed many of Prince Edward Island's finest homes and churches.

CORNELIUS HOWATT (1810-1895)

Howatt, a farmer and politician from Tryon, steadfastly opposed having Prince Edward Island join Confederation in 1873. In 1973, some Islanders who wanted to take a fresh look at the province's place in Confederation formed the Brothers and Sisters of Cornelius Howatt.

SIR ANDREW MACPHAIL (1864-1938)

His gifts as a scholar took Andrew Macphail to Charlottetown's Prince of Wales College and on to McGill University in Montreal. He became a doctor, an educator, a social critic, and a writer. His novel *The Master's Wife* told of his youth and childhood in Orwell, PEI. Today Orwell Corner itself recreates country life in the 1890s, and Macphail's house is preserved for visitors by the PEI Heritage Foundation.

LUCY MAUD MONTGOMERY (1874-1942)

Lucy Maud Montgomery lost her mother as a child. Raised by her strict grandparents in Cavendish, she found comfort in her own imagination. While still living with her invalid grandmother, she carved out a career as a writer of stories. In 1908, *Anne of Green Gables* made her internationally famous. She wrote many more novels, including the Emily of New Moon series, and she kept a vast diary that has now been published. After she married in 1911, she moved to Ontario, but her heart remained with the Island, where most of her work was set.

Anne of Green Gables' creator, Lucy Maud Montgomery.

JAMES PETERS (1811-1891)

In 1837, a young Island lawyer named James Peters married the daughter of the wealthy shipowner Samuel Cunard. In those days, the Cunard family owned one-sixth of the whole of Prince Edward Island, and Peters became the agent for the family – the rent collector, in other words. Many farm families found him a tough, hard man who was determined to collect his family's money, and rent collectors were never popular. After someone tried to burn his house down, Peters never went out without two pistols in his belt.

Province House, site of the Confederation Conference.

Prince Edward Island was named for the father of the future Queen Victoria, Prince Edward, who had served as a British military commander in Atlantic Canada. Before 1799, it was called Saint John's Island, and before that, Ile St-Jean, a name given by Jacques Cartier, who first saw the Island on the feast day of St. John the Apostle in 1534. The Mi'kmaq call the Island Abegweit, which is said to mean "cradled on the waves," or Minago.

Prince Edward Island governs itself with a legislature of thirty-two members. The Georgian-style provincial legislature, Province House, was designed by a local architect, Isaac Smith, and built with Island stone in 1843–48. As in the other provinces, the leader of the party with the largest number of elected members in the legislature becomes premier and appoints a Cabinet of ministers to run the government. The lieutenant-governor signs into law bills passed by the legislature.

Like many provinces, Prince Edward Island once had an upper house, the Legislative Council, which it later abolished. But since 1893, every riding in the province has had two members. Although one is called the assembly member and the other the councillor, they have exactly the same duties and powers.

When Prince Edward Island came into Confederation, all adult men

could vote for members of the legislature, and voting by secret ballot was soon approved. In the 1880s, however, Prince Edward Island abolished the secret ballot. Until 1913, when they got the secret ballot back, Islanders were the last voters in the country to stand up in public and shout out who they supported. Women had to wait until 1922 for the vote in provincial elections.

The province is represented in the Canadian Senate by four senators. The Canadian constitution says that no province can have fewer MPs than senators, so Islanders elect four members of Parliament to the federal House of Commons. Communities elsewhere in Canada with Prince Edward Island's population elect only one or two members to Parliament.

No Prince Edward Islander has ever been prime minister of Canada. Louis-Henry Davies, who was the Island's youngest premier in 1876, later became a Cabinet minister in Ottawa, and he was named chief justice of the Supreme Court in 1918.

JOINED CONFEDERATION:
July 1, 1873

PROVINCIAL MOTTO:
Parva sub ingenti (The small under the protection of the great)

PROVINCIAL FLOWER:
Lady's slipper

AREA:
5,660 square kilometres (by far the smallest province in Canada)

HIGHEST POINT:
Near Springton (142 metres above sea level)

POPULATION:
135,294 (55.2 per cent rural; Prince Edward Island is the least urbanized province in Canada)

GROWTH RATE:
0.5 per cent since 1996

CAPITAL:
Charlottetown

MAIN CITIES:
Charlottetown (38,114 in 2001), Summerside (14,554)

PRINCE EDWARD ISLAND GOVERNMENT INFORMATION ON THE INTERNET:
www.gov.pe.ca

THE ISLAND

Who is the great Prince Edward Island writer? Many would say Lucy
Maud Montgomery, the creator of Anne of Green Gables. You can find
"Anne" sites all over the Island. But some prefer Milton Acorn, "the
people's poet." Acorn was crabby, suspicious, and eccentric, and he
lived part of his life above a tavern in Toronto (while Lucy Maud and
her minister husband once had an elegant home a few miles away).
But Milton Acorn loved the Island as much as Montgomery did,
and he wrote some of his finest poems about it, including this one.

Since I'm Island-born home's as precise
as if a mumbly old carpenter,
shoulder-straps crossed wrong,
laid it out,
refigured to the last three-eighths of shingle.

Nowhere that plough-cut worms
heal themselves in red loam;
spruces squat, skirts in sand;
or the stones of a river rattle its dark
tunnel under the elms,
is there a spot not measured by hands;
no direction I couldn't walk
to the wave-lined edge of home.

Quiet shores – beaches that roar
but walk two thousand paces and the sea
becomes an odd shining
glimpse among the jeweled
zigzag low hills. Any wonder
your eyelashes are wings
to fly your look both in and out?
In the coves of the land all things are discussed.

In the ranged jaws of the Gulf,
a red tongue.
Indians say a musical God
took up His brush and painted it;
named it, in His own language, "The Island."

GULF OF ST. LAWRENCE

DIAN
NSULA

ADIE

IRVING

BOUCTOUCHE

NORTHUMBERLAND
STRAIT

NDE-DIGUE

MONCTON

CODIAC RIVER

MEMRAMCOOK

SACKVILLE

OF
DY

NOVA SCOTIA

BETWEEN LAND AND SEA

The Maliseet, the people of the river, have always lived along the mighty Saint John, but they haven't been alone for centuries. In the 1750s, Acadian refugees built a new home-land on the bays and coves of the Gulf of St. Lawrence. In the 1780s, American refugees founded "the Loyalist Province." In the 1840s, refugees from famine and hard-ship in Ireland also brought a new community to the province. Today descendants of all these groups, and many later immigrants, live together in New Brunswick, Canada's only officially bilingual province.

For a small province, New Brunswick has many diverse regions. Saint John has always been a busy seaport and place of business. The rich farmland of the Saint John valley, right up to Fredericton, has been the heartland of old Loyalist New Brunswick. Moncton and the nearby gulf coast have become the centre of Acadian New Brunswick, and the North Shore, a gritty, industrial region, is part Irish, part Acadian. In the northwest corner, where Maine, Quebec, and New Brunswick meet, lies the largely French-speaking "republic" of Madawaska, a region long isolated from the rest of the province.

New Brunswick is farmers, fishers, loggers, shippers, and traders. These days it looks to education too, counting on its status as one of the most bilingual parts of Canada to give it a competitive advantage.

Much of New Brunswick is what is called northern upland – rocky, hilly, and forested. The densely wooded province became known as "the timber colony" in the 1800s. Forests and minerals remain important to the province today.

Yet New Brunswick's character also comes from its great waters. The Saint John River brings rich soils to the broad farmlands along its long, fertile valley. And New Brunswick's two coastlines – one on the Bay of Fundy, one on the Gulf of St. Lawrence – have shaped the seafaring, shipping, and trading outlook of both anglophone and francophone New Brunswickers.

SAINT JOHN RIVER VALLEY

From the Bay of Fundy, you can sail ships up the Saint John River to Fredericton, in the heart of the province, and most of the way, the Saint John looks more like a lake than a river. The river has been the province's great highway since the Maliseet people first lived along it. Settlers also made their homes there, even before the Loyalists came by the thousands to found the colony of New Brunswick in the 1780s.

THE NORTH SHORE

The gulf shore is the Atlantic coast of New Brunswick. Long sand dunes shelter tidal marshes, and small harbours are crowded with fish-processing plants and fleets of fishing and scallop boats. This is the Acadian coast, and it faces Prince Edward Island, the Magdalen Islands, and Quebec's Gaspé shores, which have been populated by French-speaking Acadians since the 1760s.

The muddy residue of the Bay of Fundy at low tide.

BAY OF FUNDY

The long, narrow channel of the Bay of Fundy concentrates the highest tides in the world. What are broad expanses of deep water at high tide become vast mud flats a few hours later. The daily ebb and flow of the tides constantly nourishes the life in the abundant ecosystem of the bay – from rare right whales far out from shore to teeming microscopic life in the mud banks and salt marshes.

CENTRAL UPLANDS

In the rugged, thinly populated interior of New Brunswick stand the forests that have always generated much of the province's wealth. Once it was masts for great sailing ships that drew cutters into the woods; now it is often pulp for paper mills. Today mineral reserves beneath the soil – zinc and coal and even gold – are also being explored.

> Some of New Brunswick's rivers are privately owned. The salmon fishing is so good that all the best pools have been taken over by private clubs for sport fishermen.

MOMENTS

1866 Nowhere in British North America was Confederation debated more fiercely than in New Brunswick. In 1864, Premier Leonard Tilley thought Confederation was a great idea. But he lost the election of 1865. His anti-Confederation rival, Albert Smith, took over. Within a year, Smith's government collapsed, however, and in 1866, New Brunswick fought a second Confederation election. This time, Leonard Tilley and the pro-Confederation forces won a great victory. New Brunswick became a founding province of Canada in 1867.

1883 The *Marco Polo* was wrecked near Cavendish, Prince Edward Island. When launched at Saint John in 1851, she had been the fastest ship afloat, regularly making the quickest passages to Australia and Asia. By the 1880s, however, the day of the wooden sailing ship, the kind New Brunswickers built and sailed all over the world, was passing.

1891 Factories were expanding and New Brunswick's towns and cities were growing, but farmers were giving up and moving away – to Ontario, the United States, even Manitoba. The population barely grew for a decade.

1920 The old timber trade had faded, but in the 1920s, New Brunswick developed a new industry: pulp-and-paper manufacturing. Huge pulp mills opened on the North Shore. And during Prohibition, when alcohol was banned in the United States, another new industry blossomed in some of New Brunswick's harbours: running illegal liquor across the border.

1960 Louis Robichaud became New Brunswick's first Acadian premier. He worked to make Acadians and the French language a more vital part of New Brunswick life, and his government introduced reforms in health care, education, and industry.

A New Brunswick–built Bricklin with its "wings" up.

1970   New Brunswick tried to move into luxury carmaking with a spectacular sports car, the Bricklin, and the province invested heavily in the project. Unfortunately, the Bricklin did not catch on with buyers of expensive cars, and the cost to New Brunswickers kept going up. In the end, the Bricklin failed. Today the few that survive are collectors' items.

1987   Since 1970, Premier Richard Hatfield, a colourful bachelor lawyer, had been unbeatable in provincial politics. That ended in 1987: Hatfield's Conservatives lost every seat to the Liberal Party. The new premier, Frank McKenna, worked to build on what he called New Brunswick's special advantages for business: its low wages and low costs, its bilingual workforce, and its readiness to adopt new technology and training. McKenna held office for ten years and retired undefeated in 1997.

1999   Thirty-three-year-old Bernard Lord led his Conservative Party to victory in the provincial election, becoming one of the youngest premiers in Canadian history.

MALISEET

The Maliseet are the people of the river: they call themselves Welustuk, meaning "of the beautiful river," and they call the Saint John the Oo-lahs-took, "the good river." Today about forty-five hundred Maliseet live at Oromocto, Tobique, and other reserve communities along the river.

The coming of the Loyalists, 1783.

LOYALISTS

In 1783, thirty thousand refugees loyal to Britain fled north along the Atlantic coast from the newly independent United States. Half of them settled along the Saint John River and the Fundy shores. These lands were still part of Nova Scotia then, but the Loyalists did not want to be governed from distant Halifax. In 1784, they founded a new colony: New Brunswick (named for the British royal family of Brunswick).

Most of the Loyalists who settled in New Brunswick were ordinary farmers or working people who had been forced from their homes by the victorious American revolutionaries. But the Loyalist migration also included the families of lawyers and doctors, great landowners, and high colonial officials. They tried hard to create lives of ease and elegance in the townhouses they built in Saint John and Fredericton, and in the country estates they built along the river. Those Loyalist roots are still cherished by many New Brunswickers.

ACADIANS

Until 1755, the Acadian heartland lay in what is now Nova Scotia. Then came the great and terrible deportation, when the British expelled the French settlers. Many Acadians fled to the woods and coasts of New Brunswick. Gradually, they built a new Acadia there. Today a third of New Brunswickers are Acadians, and two-thirds of Acadians live in New Brunswick.

When they first settled in New Brunswick, the Acadians were poor refugees trying to avoid the British forces that wanted to round them up and deport them. For many years, the Acadians remained an isolated minority group within the province. In 1881, however, several of their leaders organized the first congress of Acadians at Memramcook, and they slowly began to assert themselves as a distinct community. In the 1960s, young Acadians campaigned for language rights and equal status in the province.

In 1996, New Brunswick hosted the World Congress of Acadians. Tens of thousands of Acadians and their descendants travelled to the province to celebrate Acadian culture in the region where they had once been hunted fugitives.

IRISH

In the 1830s and the 1840s, poor Irish Catholics came by the tens of thousands to Saint John, looking for a better life in North America. Many moved on, but enough stayed to change New Brunswick's population forever. No longer were the Loyalist descendants the only English-speakers in New Brunswick; no longer were the Acadians the only Catholic community in the province. Ever since, Irish-Canadian culture has been a vital element in the New Brunswick cultural mix.

POUTINE RAPÉE

A famous New Brunswick delicacy is the fiddlehead. Fiddleheads are the tender sprouts that ferns produce when they begin to grow in early May. New Brunswickers gather them in wetlands and creek banks. Lucky Canadians in the rest of the country can sometimes buy fresh or frozen New Brunswick fiddleheads, but an easier dish to make is *poutine rapée*. Acadians of the North Shore especially enjoy this dish, which is totally different from Québécois *poutine*.

8 New Brunswick potatoes
500 g (1 lb) ground beef
1 egg
1/4 cup (250 g) cream or milk

Boil four potatoes, mash, and allow to cool. Grate the other uncooked potatoes. Combine mashed and grated potatoes, and form into eight balls. Mix ground beef with egg and cream and form into eight meatballs. Insert meatballs inside potato balls and boil in water for about 30 minutes.

SAINT JOHN

Fredericton is New Brunswick's capital, but Saint John is where its trade and business go on. Here, at the mouth of the Saint John River, Mi'kmaq settlements gave way to Acadian fur-trade posts before Loyalists founded the city in 1783. After Confederation, Saint John's dream of becoming one of the great centres of Canadian industry went unfulfilled, and the city struggled for decades. Today it has been revived as a shipping and shipbuilding centre. The city core has been given new life through heritage preservation and new buildings.

Close by the heart of Saint John are the Reversing Falls. At low tide, the Saint John River plunges down through a narrow gorge into the saltwater Bay of Fundy. Then the tide rises, the flow reverses, and ocean water pours "upstream" over the gorge into the river.

Christ Church Cathedral at night.

FREDERICTON

Fredericton has always prided itself on being the centre of government, education, and culture in New Brunswick. The townsite, close by the highest navigable point on the Saint John River, had been home to Native villages and trading posts long before the Loyalists arrived in 1783. They named the site Frederick's Town, after one of the sons of King George III, and it became the capital of the new province the next year.

With just forty-four thousand people, Fredericton is one of Canada's smallest provincial capitals. But as the home of the legislative buildings, two universities, the beautiful Christ Church Cathedral, and the impressive Beaverbrook Art Gallery, Fredericton continues to play its chosen role as the heart of government and cultural life in New Brunswick.

MONCTON

Every railway line in Atlantic Canada passes through Moncton, the so-called hub of the Maritimes. Moncton has also become the centre of Acadian New Brunswick. It is home to the Université de

Moncton, as well as many Acadian businesses and arts groups. One-third French-speaking, Moncton is where you'll find most of New Brunswick's bilingual companies and services, many of which serve customers across Canada.

Visitors to Moncton can see Magnetic Hill, where cars appear to roll uphill, and the tidal bore, where the world's highest tides come racing up the Petitcodiac River.

Just outside Moncton, you can discover the optical illusion of Magnetic Hill. Park the car in neutral, take off the brake, and you will feel yourself start to roll uphill.

GRAND MANAN ISLAND

Out of the turbulent, foggy waters of the Bay of Fundy rise the cliffs and headlands of Grand Manan, the largest of New Brunswick's off-shore islands. A fishing port for generations, Grand Manan is also a seabird sanctuary and a prime site for whale watching. Residents of Grand Manan harvest and market dulse, an edible seaweed still enjoyed as a salty snack by many Maritimers.

Fog at Grand Manan Island.

NEW BRUNSWICK AT WORK

PHONE CENTRE WORKERS

In the 1980s and the 1990s, New Brunswickers began to see technology, education, and bilingualism as assets they could use to their advantage. The most heavily populated parts of Canada may be far away, but with computer and telephone networks, no place is remote, and New Brunswick plans to benefit from the business opportunities that new technologies create. Today many of the bilingual call centres – the places Canadians reach through an 800 phone number for services or information – are staffed by young New Brunswickers, often in Moncton.

SHIPBUILDERS

A nineteenth-century schooner under construction.

In 1851, the shipbuilders of New Brunswick built the *Marco Polo*, the biggest, fastest, and (they said) most beautiful ship afloat. In fact, in the

mid-1800s, hundreds of wooden ships and schooners were launched from New Brunswick ports, and Saint John was one of Canada's busiest seaports.

The great days of sail eventually ended, but shipbuilding has continued. From 1914 to the 1950s, the Saint John dry dock, where ships are repaired, was the largest in the world. In the 1990s, ship-builders at Saint John built and launched several new frigates for the Canadian navy.

PULP-AND-PAPER WORKERS

New Brunswick has been a timber province for two hundred years. At one time, loggers cut tall pine masts for sailing ships. Today pulp-and-paper milling is a vital industry. Mills at Saint John, Bathurst, Newcastle, Campbellton, Edmundston, Dalhousie, and other centres are an important source of work and income for people in the province.

WHALE SCIENTISTS

A small population of rare right whales, once hunted almost to extinction, now spends part of the year feeding in the food-rich waters of the Bay of Fundy. Too much attention is dangerous for them, but science may be able to help save their lives and rebuild their numbers. To learn more about them, dedicated whale scientists follow them in small boats, adding patiently to a vital database of knowledge of these great sea mammals.

MAX AITKEN (1879-1964)

Max Aitken was a salesman; he could sell anything. Moving restlessly from New Brunswick to Calgary to Montreal, he built a financial empire in Canada. Then he moved to Britain, where he became an influential politician and later a "press baron," the owner of some of Britain's leading newspapers. But he did not forget his home. When he was appointed to the British House of Lords, with the title Baron Beaverbrook (which he chose to commemorate a stream near his birthplace), he started to make lavish donations to his native province, including the funds that established Fredericton's Beaverbrook Art Gallery.

BLISS CARMAN (1861-1929)

Could you become a writer if you were born in Fredericton in the middle of the 1800s? Bliss Carman proved you could. He wrote for newspapers and magazines in Canada and the United States, and his poems on Canadian themes were very popular. "Low Tide at Grand Pré," which he wrote in 1893, remained a cornerstone of Canadian poetry collections for decades. For a time, he and his cousin Charles G. D. Roberts, also from New Brunswick, were two of Canada's best-known and most respected writers.

ALEX COLVILLE (1920-   )

Alex Colville became a realist painter even when abstract painting was the fashion. He settled into Sackville, New Brunswick, to do so, and for many years, he taught art at Mount Allison University there. You can always identify the people, animals, and objects in Colville paintings, but they are never simply photographic. There is always something more going on. Some people call the kind of painting he does magic realism, and he is recognized the world over as one of the best at it. Though he was born in Toronto and has lived in Nova Scotia since 1971, he remains associated with Sackville.

KENNETH C. IRVING (1899-1992)

Starting with a gas station in small-town Bouctouche, K. C. Irving expanded his commercial empire until it seemed he owned most of New Brunswick. Irving's companies ran the province's newspapers and TV stations, its gas stations, its timber lots, its pulp mills, even its bus

The only person from "the colonies" to become prime minister of Great Britain was Andrew Bonar Law, a minister's son from rural New Brunswick, who was Britain's prime minister for a few months in 1922–23.

lines. Irving became one of the richest men in the world, and he was also one of the most controversial people in New Brunswick because of his power and influence.

ANTONINE MAILLET (1929-   )

Antonine Maillet is a storyteller who has become the voice of Acadia. Her play *La Sagouine*, about a talkative Acadian cleaning lady, made her a legend among French-speaking Canadians. *Pélagie-la-Charrette*, a novel about the Acadians who returned from exile after the great deportation of 1755, made her world famous when it won France's prestigious Prix Goncourt.

LOUIS ROBICHAUD (1925-   )

Louis Robichaud, an Acadian from Kent County, one of New Brunswick's poorest regions, became premier in 1960. He modernized New Brunswick and its government so thoroughly that his ten years in power became known as the Robichaud Revolution. Above all, he guaranteed his fellow Acadians a strong and permanent place in New Brunswick's politics and society.

LEONARD TILLEY (1818-1896)

Would New Brunswick accept this idea of Confederation that was in the air in the 1860s? Premier Leonard Tilley believed it should. In 1865, he staked his government on the question – and lost the election. But Tilley did not despair. A year later, New Brunswick held another election on the Confederation question, and this time he won. Confederation went ahead.

Tilley started his career as a pharmacist's apprentice in rural New Brunswick, and he became New Brunswick's most successful politician. He served as provincial premier, as a powerful Cabinet minister in Ottawa, and finally as lieutenant-governor of the province. One of the things he believed in was temperance: he never drank liquor, and he believed it should be banned. But when he tried to pass temperance laws in 1855, New Brunswickers threw his government out of office.

Premier Leonard Tilley, a powerful voice for Confederation.

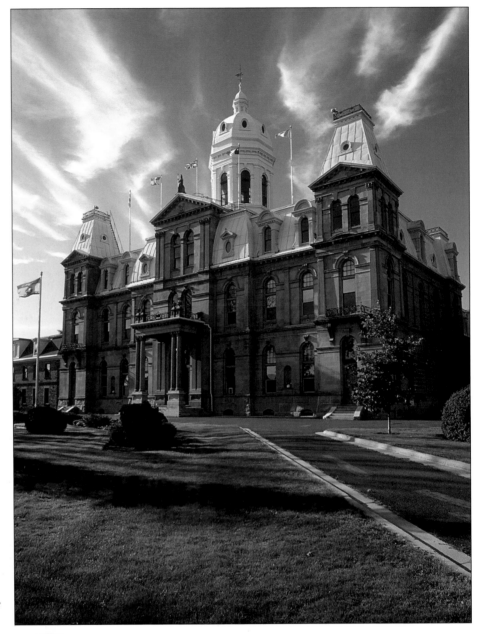

The ornate provincial legislature at Fredericton.

New Brunswickers govern themselves through a legislature of fifty-eight seats. The leader of the party with the greatest number of members becomes the premier and appoints a Cabinet of ministers to run the government. The lieutenant-governor signs into law bills passed by the legislature. The legislature building, located at Fredericton, was designed by the Saint John architect James Dumaresq in the French Second Empire style. It's topped by a British cupola and a statue of Britannia, and it opened in 1882.

In Ottawa, New Brunswickers are represented by ten members of Parliament and ten senators. New Brunswick was one of the first

Canadian provinces to give all men the vote. Women first got the vote there in 1919.

In the 1987 election, the Liberal Party of Frank McKenna won every seat in the legislature. But New Brunswickers have supported both Liberal and Conservative premiers over the years. In 1999, Bernard Lord led the Conservative Party to victory and became premier. He was just thirty-three years old, making him one of the youngest premiers in Canadian history.

No New Brunswicker has been prime minister of Canada while representing a New Brunswick constituency. Richard B. Bennett (who was prime minister from 1930 to 1935) was born in Hopewell Hill, New Brunswick, and started his law career in Chatham before moving to Alberta.

BILINGUALISM IN NEW BRUNSWICK

New Brunswick is also Nouveau-Brunswick. Since the 1960s, when the first Acadian premier, Louis Robichaud, took office, the province has proudly been making itself into a place where both French and English are used and respected.

In the 1960s and 1970s, New Brunswickers sometimes had angry debates about the role of Acadians and their French language in the life of the province. There were stormy confrontations in Moncton, the city where French- and English-speakers are most mixed together. But two pre-miers, Louis Robichaud and Richard Hatfield – one French-speaking, one English-speaking – helped New Brunswickers begin to recognize the needs and the rights of both of its leading languages and cultural communities. Since it passed its Official Languages Act in 1969, New Brunswick has been Canada's only officially bilingual province.

Not everyone speaks both languages, of course. Many parts of the North Shore are very French, while the lower Saint John River valley is very English. Still, the province's ability to work in two languages is more and more often recognized as an asset, not a problem. The rich Acadian heritage is now an hon-oured part of the province's cultural mix. New Brunswick's Acadian musicians, writers, and actors are admired and celebrated all over Canada.

Canada's first Acadian premier, Louis Robichaud.

JOINED CONFEDERATION:
July 1, 1867

PROVINCIAL MOTTO:
Spem reduxit (Hope was restored)

PROVINCIAL FLOWER:
Purple violet

AREA:
73,436 square kilometres

HIGHEST POINT:
Mount Carleton (820 metres above sea level)

POPULATION:
729,498 (49 per cent urban, 51 per cent rural;
64 per cent English, 32 per cent French)

GROWTH RATE:
Down 1.2 per cent since 1996

CAPITAL:
Fredericton

MAIN CITIES:
Saint John (122,678 in 2001), Moncton (90,359),
Fredericton (54,068), Bathurst (16,427)

**NEW BRUNSWICK GOVERNMENT INFORMATION
ON THE INTERNET:**
www.gov.nb.ca

James De Mille was a serious teacher and professor at Dalhousie
University in Halifax. He was also a very successful popular novelist,
known all over North America in the late 1800s. But he was always a
New Brunswicker at heart, and once in a while he wrote silly songs and
poems about his home province – like this one about its remarkable
place names.

Sweet maiden of Passamaquoddy,
Shall we seek for communion of souls
Where the deep Mississippi meanders,
Or the distant Saskatchewan rolls?
Ah no, in New Brunswick we'll find it –
A sweetly sequestered nook –
Where the sweet gliding Skoodawabskooksis
Unites with the Skoodawabskook . . .

Let others sing loudly of Saco,
Of Passadumkeag or Miscouche,
Of the Kennebecasis or Quaco,
Of Miramichi or Buctouche;
Or boast of the Tobique or Mispec,
The Mushquash or dark
Memramcook;
There's none like the
Skoodawabskooksis
Excepting the
Skoodawabskook.

QUEBEC

BARREN GROUNDS

HUDSON BAY

UNGAVA BAY

UNGAVA PENINSULA

JAMES BAY

LABRADOR

ONTARIO

CHIBOUGAMAU

MANICOUAGAN RIVER

SEPT-ÎLES

ANTI...
...S

BAIE-COMEAU

ST. LAWRENCE RIVER

ROUYN-NORANDA

JONQUIÈRE

SAGUENAY RIVER

RIMOUSKI

GASPÉ PENINSULA

CHICOUTIMI

QUEBEC CITY

NEW BRUNSWICK

SHAWINIGAN

HULL

TROIS-RIVIÈRES

MONTREAL

A DISTINCT SOCIETY

C'est une province pas comme les autres. It's a province not like any other.

Quebec is Canada's largest province in area and its second largest in population. It is the heartland of French-speaking civilization in North America, and that makes it special. French Quebec is a society more than three hundred years old. Quebec is proud of its heritage – and just as proud of its determination to control its own destiny. Quebeckers rarely forget those facts.

For a century and a half, Quebec was New France, a French colony that came to dominate half of North America. New France was conquered by the British in 1763, but French Quebec survived under British rule. .

During the 1800s, English settlers began to dominate the cities and take the lead in industry and finance. French Quebeckers seemed destined to be poor farmers and woodcutters in the countryside. But the 1960s saw the resurgence of French Quebec. It became modern and diverse, a lively urban culture active in all aspects of the province's life.

Since the 1960s, the growing confidence of French Quebec has been accompanied by a revival of Quebec nationalism, as Quebeckers debate whether they would be better off as a nation of their own. Whatever its future, the province has been a vital part of Canada. Many of the great events of Canadian history have occurred there, and without Quebec, Canada would have evolved as a very different society. The province is the home to large English-speaking populations, proud Native nations, and thriving immigrant communities that speak both French and English, as well as their own languages. Quebec is a key source of the liveliness and diversity of Canadian life.

Four-fifths of Quebec (which is Canada's largest province and covers more than 15 per cent of the country) lies on the Canadian Shield, the land of rock and lakes and forest. The northernmost parts of Quebec are treeless Barren Grounds by the Hudson Strait. Far to the south stand the hardwood forests that provide Quebec's blazing fall colours and most of the world's maple syrup.

ST. LAWRENCE VALLEY

The St. Lawrence was born as the great glaciers melted about ten thousand years ago; it drained glacial meltwater from the centre of North America. Today the St. Lawrence carries ten thousand square metres of water every second, making it one of the world's largest rivers, though it's far from the longest. Using the river, the Great Lakes, and the Gulf of St. Lawrence, sailors can travel almost four thousand kilometres into North America from the open Atlantic.

Since the days of the Iroquoian farmers, the narrow, fertile river valley has been home to most of the people of Quebec. For Quebeckers, the St. Lawrence is simply *le fleuve*, the river.

CANADIAN SHIELD COUNTRY

Not far north of the St. Lawrence begins the Canadian Shield. At first, it is a land of lakes and rivers and forests. On the east, at Manicouagan, and to the west, on the James Bay shore, great rivers have been dammed for hydroelectric power. Farther north, towards the Hudson Strait, lies the barren treeless tundra. This rugged region, home to the Cree, the Inuit, and the Innu, is where you'll find caribou herds and roaming polar bears. This part of the Canadian Shield is some of the oldest rock in the world, and it has been repeatedly ground down

by glaciation. Many geologists argue that somewhere in this barren landscape there should be a source of diamonds, but if there is, it is as yet undiscovered.

*The Saguenay Fjord is
Canada's southernmost fjord.*

MONTEREGIAN HILLS

Volcanoes once erupted on the broad plain around Montreal. Today only their hardened cores remain, and they form Mount Royal, on whose slopes Montreal stands, and several other hills across the river south of the city.

Farther east, the Appalachians, the worn-down ancient mountains that form the spine of the eastern United States, reach up into Quebec. They provide the backbone of the rugged Gaspé Peninsula.

SAGUENAY FJORD

The spectacular Saguenay Fjord is the only place outside the Arctic where the white beluga whale lives. The Saguenay River flows to the St. Lawrence from Lac St-Jean through a deep gash in the earth's crust. When Jacques Cartier visited in 1535, he heard that the river led to an area called the Kingdom of the Saguenay, and he hoped that France might find rich cities and empires to conquer there. Cartier never found the kingdom, but the name is still used for the vast region drained by this river.

1865   "French Canadians are a separate people," said Hector Langevin, one of Quebec's political leaders, in 1865. They would join Confederation only if they were sure their language, culture, and religion were secure. Despite opposition, Quebec's representatives decided in favour of Confederation in 1867.

1887   The politician Honoré Mercier was elected premier of Quebec. Though he stayed in power only a few years, he was Quebec's first strong and popular premier. He argued that his government had a role different from that of any other provincial government, because it was the government of the Quebec nation. Only the provincial government could truly speak for French Quebec, he said.

Quebeckers turned out in force to protest conscription in 1917.

1917   With the First World War in its third year, the Canadian government decided it had to conscript soldiers (that is, take young men into the army whether they wanted to fight or not). But many Quebeckers had not wanted to take part in what they considered England's war, and they were even more strongly opposed to conscription. When a mostly English-Canadian coalition in Parliament imposed conscription against Quebec's wishes, many French Canadians protested violently. For decades, Quebeckers felt a lasting resentment.

1944   Maurice Duplessis – whom everyone called *le chef* (the boss) – was re-elected premier after a few years out of power. He would stay in office for fifteen more years. A powerful, bullying politician who seemed to control everyone and everything in his province, Duplessis was often in conflict with the government in Ottawa as he fought to defend Quebec's powers. Premier Duplessis resisted changes in French-Canadian society, and today his time is sometimes remembered as the *grand noirceur*, the great darkness.

1960   The Révolution tranquille, the Quiet Revolution, was the sudden change that created modern, prosperous, fashionable Quebec. Quebeckers had always looked to their Catholic religion and their traditional farming way of life to protect them from the English-speaking Protestant world around them. But by 1960, most Quebeckers lived in cities and worked in office and factories. They

began to look less to the Catholic Church to guide them – and to rethink Quebec's place in Canada.

1967 Fifty million people flocked to Montreal to celebrate Canada's centennial at Expo 67.

1970 Would Quebec remain part of Canada or become an independent state? And how would the decision be made? In October 1970, the terrorists of the FLQ (the Front de Libération du Québec) decided that kidnapping was the way to bring about the "liberation" of the province. When they seized two hostages, Prime Minister Pierre Trudeau sent troops to Montreal. During what came to be called the October Crisis, the kidnappers killed one of their victims, the Quebec Cabinet minister Pierre Laporte. Some of the kidnappers were eventually captured and jailed, but others went into exile in Cuba. Disgusted by the violence, Quebeckers made sure that whatever future the province chose, it would be decided peacefully.

1980 In 1976, the Parti Québécois, a political party committed to the independence of Quebec, won the provincial election. In 1980, Premier René Lévesque asked Quebeckers to vote yes or no on his plan for "sovereignty-association" – an independent Quebec with links to Canada. Sixty per cent of Quebeckers said no.

The War Measures Act brought troops to the streets of Montreal in 1970.

1982 Prime Minister Trudeau, a Quebecker, patriated the Canadian Constitution and added to it a Charter of Rights and Freedoms. But Quebec had opposed Trudeau's changes, and so the Constitution came to Canada without Quebec's support.

1995 When Canadian leaders were unsuccessful at attempts to devise constitutional changes Quebec would approve, the province held a second sovereignty referendum in October 1995. This time the results were very close, but once more the federalist side won: a handful more voters said no than said yes.

QUÉBÉCOIS

Eighty per cent of the people of Quebec are French-speakers, and most of these are descendants of a few thousand settlers who came to New France in the 1600s and 1700s. The francophone people of Quebec have a deep sense of themselves as a unique community. Today, however, French Quebec is growing more diverse. Quebec now attracts francophone immigrants from Africa and the Caribbean, and more non-francophone Quebeckers have learned the language and joined in francophone life.

CREE

The Cree occupy a vast stretch of boreal forest across northern Canada. The easternmost Cree territory lies on the James Bay shore of northern Quebec. In 1975, Quebec, Canada, and the Cree of James Bay signed the James Bay Agreement. It permitted hydroelectric development of the James Bay rivers, but it also recognized the Cree territories and their rights to self-government.

A Mohawk warrior and a Canadian soldier face off during the Oka dispute.

MOHAWK

In the 1600s, the Mohawk and other members of what was called the Five Nations (or Iroquois) Confederacy were fierce rivals of New France and its Native allies, the Montagnais and Huron nations. Despite this rivalry, some Mohawk from the Five Nations became Catholics and moved to lands near Montreal. Ever since, a strong, proud Mohawk nation has lived within the borders of Quebec, and today there are several Mohawk reserves around Montreal. In 1990, disputes over the use of Mohawk land near Oka led to an armed confrontation between Mohawk warriors, Quebec police, and Canadian soldiers.

MONTAGNAIS

The French word *montagnais* means "highlander." The Montagnais are the Algonquian-speaking peoples who lived by hunting, gathering, and trading in the rugged country north of the Gulf of St. Lawrence. Today they continue to live along the North Shore.

ANGLO-QUEBECKERS

During the eighteenth and nineteenth centuries, settlers from Britain poured into Quebec. Quebec City and Montreal, as well as regions like the Eastern Townships and the Gaspé Peninsula, became heavily

English-speaking. Today Anglo-Quebeckers are much more likely to speak French, but they continue to assert that they have deep roots and are full partners in Quebec life.

ALLOPHONES

All through the twentieth century, non-English, non-French immigrants came to Canada. Particularly in Montreal, immigrants who are neither French nor English in origin, called allophones, have become an important part of the local community. Today many newcomers become trilingual – speaking their own language, as well as English and French.

JEWS

Between about 1880 and 1910, tens of thousands of Jews migrated to Canada, often fleeing persecution in eastern Europe. The largest number settled in Montreal. Though many of them were very poor, their children succeeded rapidly in business, medicine, law, education, and the arts, despite having to fight prejudice from both anglophone and francophone Quebeckers. Today eastern European Jewish favourites such as bagels and smoked meat have become "traditional" Montreal products.

> Over the years, many British immigrants assimilated into French-speaking Quebec. Today there are French Quebeckers who have surnames like O'Neill, Ryan, Jones, and MacLean.

TOURTIÈRE

Tourtière used to be pigeon (*tourte*) pie. Today it is a meat pie, usually made with pork or veal. Quebeckers love to argue about the ingredients of the true tourtière, which is served at the midnight meal called *réveillon* on Christmas Eve.

1 1/2 lb (750 g) ground lean pork
1 small onion, minced
1/2 cup (125 mL) boiling water
1 garlic clove, chopped
1 1/2 tsp (7 mL) salt
1/4 tsp (1 mL) celery salt
1/4 tsp (1 mL) black pepper
1/4 tsp (1 mL) sage
pinch of ground cloves

Combine all ingredients in a heavy 3-quart (3 L) saucepan. Cook over low heat, stirring constantly, until meat loses its red colour and about half the liquid has evaporated. Cover and cook about 45 minutes longer.

Meanwhile, boil and mash three medium-sized potatoes. Mix mashed potatoes into cooked meat mixture, then cool. Prepare enough pastry for two 9-inch (23 cm) pie crusts. Place half the dough into a 9-inch (23 cm) pie plate and fill with meat mixture. Use the remainder of the dough to cover the pie, sealing the edges and slashing the top crust. Bake in a preheated 450°F (230°C) oven for 10 minutes, then reduce heat to 350°F (180°C) and bake another 30 to 40 minutes until done.

Quebec City stands sentinel over the St. Lawrence.

QUEBEC CITY

In the Algonquian language, Quebec means "where the river narrows." The city on the cliffs, founded in 1608 at the site of an older Native town, has always controlled events along the river. Quebec City is one of the oldest and most beautiful cities in North America, as well as one of the coldest and snowiest. Thousands of visitors enjoy its annual Winter Carnival, with its ice sculptures, iceboat races on the frozen river, and Bonhomme, the festival mascot.

MONTREAL

Montreal was founded as a religious mission in 1642, but it soon began to prosper because of the fur trade. Montreal merchants dominated that industry until the 1820s. By then, Montreal was Canada's largest city and the centre of trade, transportation, and industry. Today it shares those roles with Toronto, but it remains the greatest French city in North America. It is the centre of French Quebec's cultural and intellectual life, and it also has a lively bilingual and multicultural personality.

HULL

Hull was born as a lumbering centre beside the rapids of the Ottawa River. In the 1800s, it was a rough, brawling, noisy city, where French, Irish, and American lumbermen often caroused and fought. Today Hull is part of the National Capital Region of Ottawa-Hull. Its riverfront is crowded with government offices and magnificent attractions such as the Canadian Museum of Civilization.

ROUYN-NORANDA

The twin cities of Rouyn-Noranda were born from Quebec's gold- and copper-mining boom of the 1920s, and they grew into the largest cities in northwest Quebec. Rouyn is named for a soldier in the wars of New France. Noranda, a name chosen by a mining company, combines the words *north* and *Canada*.

The fabled Saguenay River.

THE KINGDOM OF THE SAGUENAY

When the farming territories along the St. Lawrence River became crowded in the late 1800s, a few pioneers ventured north, to the lands of the Saguenay valley around Lac St-Jean. The Saguenay region grew rapidly, and logging, industry, and power dams became as important as farming. The people of the Saguenay still consider themselves pioneers of a frontier region and guardians of the language and traditions of old Quebec.

RICHELIEU VALLEY

Today the Richelieu River flows peacefully amid apple orchards and prosperous farms from Lake Champlain and the United States towards the St. Lawrence. But forts, museums, and battlefield parks recall how the valley has often been the site of wars. French settlers fought the Mohawk in the 1600s. British, French, and American armies clashed during the 1700s, and Patriotes defeated British troops at St-Denis-sur-Richelieu in the rebellion of 1837–38. Collège militaire St-Jean, one of Canada's two military colleges, is located at St-Jean-sur-Richelieu. Today canal locks welcome recreational boaters to this picturesque district.

PERFORMERS

In the 1960s, the traditional culture of French Quebec gave birth to vibrant new artists, singers, writers, and film-makers. Today such Quebeckers are famous all over the French-speaking world. French stars like Céline Dion often "cross over" into English as well. Cirque du Soleil, one of North America's most successful circuses, was founded by Quebec street performers.

HYDROELECTRIC WORKERS

In the 1960s, Hydro-Quebec began building huge power dams on many of Quebec's wild rivers. The dams became a symbol of the new, modern, powerful Quebec. One of the first big power dams, on the Manicouagan River, was the subject of a popular folk song, "La Manic."

In the 1970s and 1980s, the James Bay Project became one of the largest power developments ever attempted. Whole river systems in northern Quebec were diverted. Spillways larger than Niagara Falls were cut out of bedrock. By the 1990s, however, power dams were controversial. For some years, conservation groups and Cree activists prevented a second stage of the James Bay Project from going ahead.

MAPLE SUGAR PRODUCERS

Native peoples taught settlers how to gather sweet sap from the maple trees along the St. Lawrence and boil it down into syrup and sugar. Ever since, Quebec has been the largest maple-syrup producer in the world. Collecting maple syrup used to be a matter of hanging a bucket on a tree, collecting sap, and boiling it over an open fire. Today commercial sugarbushes draw sap from hundreds of trees through suction hoses.

DRAVEURS

All through the 1800s and 1900s, logging was one of Quebec's most important industries. Thousands of Quebeckers went every winter to "shanties" in the woods to cut down trees. The *draveurs* (log drivers),

Unlike English Canadians, francophone Quebeckers mostly watch television programs made in their own province.

The draveurs *became a folk symbol of Quebec.*

who guided logs down the rivers to the mills or to timber ships waiting on the St. Lawrence, gradually joined the fur trade's voyageurs as heroes of Quebec's folk songs and stories.

SOFTWARE EN FRANÇAIS

Are all the world's computers going to speak English? Montreal is one of the key places where French-language software is being developed. Because it's a North American city, Montreal is in touch with the latest computer developments. Because it's a French city, it has what it takes to develop computer tools that can cross language barriers.

THÉRÈSE CASGRAIN (1896-1981)

Working for change was not easy in traditional Quebec. Many of Thérèse Casgrain's well-to-do relatives and friends were shocked when she began campaigning for women's rights, and it took twenty years for women to gain the right to vote in Quebec. Eventually, Casgrain became a popular radio host, a political leader, and a campaigner for peace and rights. In 1970, she was appointed to the Senate.

CÉLINE DION (1968-   )

The youngest of fourteen children, Céline Dion began her career as a child pop singer, loved in Quebec but unknown beyond. Gradually, her popularity grew in French-speaking countries. She released her first English-language recording in 1990, and by the end of the 1990s, she was the most successful and popular female singer in the world.

RENÉ LÉVESQUE (1922-1987)

René Lévesque was a popular broadcaster and politician when he decided in the 1960s that Quebec had to pursue its future outside of Canada. Quebeckers elected him their premier in 1976, but after a hard-fought referendum, they turned down his plan for independence in 1980. Yet Lévesque continued to be warmly admired for his passion and his commitment to justice and democracy for all.

René Lévesque is besieged by reporters after the first Parti Québecois election victory on November 16, 1976.

DONALD MORRISON (1858-1894)

Born among the poor Scottish settlers of Megantic in southeastern Quebec, Donald Morrison fought with the wealthy investor who had taken over his family's farm, and in 1888 he killed a policeman sent to arrest him. For nearly a year, Morrison hid out in the woods, protected by sympathetic neighbours and relatives. The Megantic Outlaw, as he was known, died in prison after being captured, but he lived on as a legend among the people of his region.

LOUIS-JOSEPH PAPINEAU (1786-1871)

In the 1830s, Louis-Joseph Papineau and his followers, called the Patriotes, grew frustrated with the power of Quebec's British governor, with the floods of English-speaking immigrants, and with the hard times afflicting French Quebec. In 1837 and 1838, the Patriotes rose in unsuccessful rebellions. Although Papineau had to go into exile for several years, he remains a hero to many Quebeckers, who view him as the first person to fight for an independent Quebec.

MAURICE "ROCKET" RICHARD (1921-2000)

Quebec has given the world scores of hockey heroes, but none could ever quite match the impact of the Rocket. As the leader of the Montreal Canadiens, Maurice Richard always seemed able to score the winning goal at the crucial moment. Richard held all the records of pro hockey when he retired in 1960.

The Rocket, Jean Béliveau, and Gordie Howe in action.

MORDECAI RICHLER (1931-2001)

A poor boy from Montreal's Jewish community, Mordecai Richler made himself an internationally known novelist, screenwriter, and magazine journalist. Richler was a proud Canadian and a proud Montrealer, but not a sentimental one. In his writing, he often mocked Canadian pretensions, and he spoke out against Quebec's restrictive language laws and other attempts to encourage French-language culture.

PIERRE TRUDEAU (1919-2000)

Brilliant, opinionated, and always inclined to follow his own path, Pierre Trudeau decided to go to Ottawa in the 1960s, when most Quebeckers were looking more to their provincial capital in Quebec City. Trudeau soon became one of Canada's most colourful and successful prime ministers. He always argued that Quebec would fulfil its destiny not through independence, but as part of a bilingual, bicultural Canada.

JACQUES VILLENEUVE (1971-   )

Quebecker Gilles Villeneuve, winner of the Montreal Grand Prix, was Canada's finest racing-car driver until he was killed in an accident in Belgium in 1982. In the 1990s, his son, Jacques, had even greater success in the same sport. In 1998, Jacques became world racing champion – a hero in Quebec and around the world. His place as one of the international celebrities of this thrilling and risky sport is secure

Quebec City's imposing Assemblée Nationale.

Before 1867, it had been called Canada East (1841–67), Lower Canada (1791–1841), Quebec (1763–91), and New France (until 1763).

Quebeckers govern themselves through a legislature of 122 seats, the Assemblée Nationale, in Quebec City. The leader of the party with the greatest number of members (called MNAs, members of the National Assembly) serves as premier and chooses a Cabinet of ministers to run the government. The lieutenant-governor signs into law bills passed by the legislature.

The Assemblée Nationale, designed by Étienne Taché, was built in 1877–87, just outside the walls of old Quebec. It was designed in the Second Empire style, which was then fashionable in France but less familiar in North America.

In the Canadian Parliament in Ottawa, Quebeckers are represented by seventy-five members. Quebec's representation is fixed (first at sixty-five, now seventy-five), while the number of MPs from other provinces changes as the populations of those provinces change in relation to Quebec's. Quebec also has twenty-four senators in Ottawa. Many Quebeckers have played prominent roles in Canadian political

life. Seven of the first twenty Canadian prime ministers have been
Quebeckers, including Sir Wilfrid Laurier, Pierre Elliott Trudeau, and
Brian Mulroney. Quebec's provincial premiers have also been national
figures on many occasions.

The battle over separatism pitted neighbours – and even family members – against each other.

THE SEPARATION QUESTION

Politics in Quebec has always been about the future of *la nation
québécoise*. Quebeckers have always played a vital part in the political
life of Canada, but most believe their provincial government has a special
role as the national government of Quebec, a society with its own
language, legal code, history, and culture.

Since the 1970s, separatists (or sovereigntists) have argued that
Quebec should no longer remain a province of Canada. They believe
it should be an independent, sovereign country, probably with some
economic association with Canada. Those who support the opposing
view, known as federalists, argue that Quebeckers can preserve their
distinctive ways while remaining partners in the Canadian nation. The
debate among nationalists, separatists, and federalists has kept Quebec
politics lively for many decades.

QUEBEC AT A GLANCE

JOINED CONFEDERATION:
July 1, 1867

PROVINCIAL MOTTO:
Je me souviens (I remember)

PROVINCIAL FLOWER:
Fleur de lis (Madonna lily)

AREA:
1,540,000 square kilometres (largest of the provinces)

HIGHEST POINT:
Mont d'Iberville (1,652 metres above sea level)

POPULATION:
7,237,497 (more than 80 per cent francophone)

GROWTH RATE:
1.4 per cent since 1996

CAPITAL:
Quebec City

MAIN CITIES:
Quebec (635,184), Montreal (3,215,665 in 2001),
Sherbrooke (127,354), Hull (66,246), Trois-Rivières (117,758)

QUEBEC GOVERNMENT INFORMATION ON THE INTERNET:
www.gov.qc.ca

TWO STRONG MEN
JOSEPH MONTFERRAND & LOUIS CYR

Traditionally, Quebeckers were hard workers in tough jobs. They admired strong, agile men, whose feats of strength made all francophones feel stronger. Two of Quebec's greatest strongmen were Joseph Montferrand and Louis Cyr. One became a legend in the 1800s, and the other became a world record holder in the 1900s.

Joseph Montferrand was one of the strongest men around Montreal in the 1820s and 1830s – a wagon driver, a voyageur, and a boxing champion. When he became a woodsman, he grew even more famous. Soon, he was the king of the Ottawa River loggers – men who were celebrated for their strength, their courage, and their wild exploits – and the man everyone up and down the river told stories about. Before he died in 1864, he was one of the most famous men in Quebec.

In the stories people liked to tell, Montferrand the legend could leap in the air, leave his bootprints on a tavern ceiling, and land safely on his feet. He could throw heavy iron ploughs around or fight fifty Irish loggers and win. Of course, he also cut more trees and steered more rafts through more rapids than anyone else.

After Montferrand's death, all kinds of legends began to be attached to his name. In English, "Joe Mufferaw" stories, based on Montferrand's exploits, travelled to the forests of Maine, Michigan, and Wisconsin, and across western Canada.

But Joseph Montferrand wasn't Quebec's only beloved strongman. Louis Cyr was born about the time Montferrand died. He was not tall, but he was huge and very strong. One day, he lifted a horse just to impress his friends.

Sometimes Louis Cyr worked as a policeman, but he also travelled the world with the Ringling Brothers and Barnum and Bailey circuses and with his own Troupe Cyr, amazing crowds and challenging anyone to match his feats of strength.

And what were some of those feats? Once, Cyr lifted 250 kilograms with one finger. With one hand, he lifted 124 kilograms over his head. He even hoisted a platform carrying eighteen fat men and weighing 1,967 kilograms, still believed to be the most weight ever lifted by one man. No challenger ever beat the world's strongest man.

ONTARIO

HUDSON BAY

MANITOBA

POLAR
BEAR
PROVINCIAL
PARK

JAMES BAY

MOOSONEE

KENORA

LAKE
NIPIGON

LAKE
OF THE
WOODS

TIMMINS

THUNDER BAY

WAWA

LAKE SUPERIOR

SUDBURY

NORTH
BAY

LAKE
NIPIS

SAULT STE MARIE

U.S.A.

MANITOULIN
ISLAND

GEORGIAN
BAY

TOBERMO

OSHAWA

COLLINGWOO

LAKE
HURON

TORONTO

NIAGARA ESCARP

LAKE ONTARIO

KITCHENER

STRATFORD

HAMILTON

NIAGARA
FALLS

S
TOR

THAMES RIVER

GRAND RIVER

LAKE
ST CLAIR

LONDON

BRANTFORD

U.S.A.

LAKE E

WINDSOR

WELLAND

POINT PELEE

QUEBEC

OTTAWA
TAWA RIVER

KINGSTON
ETERBOROUGH
ARIO

STILL THE KEYSTONE OF CANADA?

I n 1867, the year of Confederation, Ontario already had the most people and the greatest wealth of any Canadian province. For the next century, Ontario made itself the centre of Canadian political, economic, and cultural life.

That had all happened very quickly. In the 1780s, Ontario had simply been the "upper" part of Canada, the barely settled backwoods of British North America. But then came American Loyalists, soon to be joined by British settlers, and they filled the abundant farmland in the region between Lake Ontario and Lake Huron. As it expanded, Ontario developed forestry, mining, hydroelectricity, and other resources. Factories and industries bloomed in southern towns, and Toronto began to compete with Montreal to be Canada's largest city.

Ontario was very British by the end of the 1800s, though there were large Franco-Ontarian communities in the east and north. In the 1900s, immigrants from the rest of the world changed Ontario permanently. Today its cities are some of the most multicultural places in the world. Over the years, waves of Jewish, Ukrainian, Italian, Portuguese, Asian, Jamaican, East Indian, and Somali immigrants have each added their special contribution.

At the start of the twenty-first century, Ontario is still large, prosperous, and diverse. But the other regions of Canada have also grown in size and confidence. They have their own strengths and ambitions, for themselves and for Canada. None of them admits that Ontario must always be the Canadian leader in all things. Will Ontario still be able to think of itself as the centre of Canada – or will it become just a province like the others?

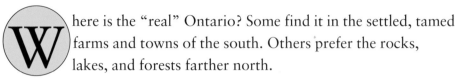

**Point Pelee
is as far south as
California and Spain.**

Where is the "real" Ontario? Some find it in the settled, tamed farms and towns of the south. Others prefer the rocks, lakes, and forests farther north.

North to south, Ontario stretches from the polar bear country by Hudson Bay to the grapevines of Pelee Island, the most southerly part of Canada. East to west, it covers more than twenty-five degrees of latitude, from the rocky Thousand Islands across rich farmland to the boreal forest north of Lake of the Woods.

SOUTHERN ONTARIO FARMLAND

Sir John Graves Simcoe, the lieutenant-governor who founded the colony called Upper Canada in 1792, predicted "that great peninsula between the lakes Huron, Erie, and Ontario" was "destined by nature, sooner or later, to govern the interior" of North America. Southern Ontario never became that powerful, but barely seventy-five years after Simcoe's prediction, the new province of Ontario had more than a million people.

Most of them lived on "that great peninsula." Southern Ontario has thousands of square kilometres of rich, rolling farmland, from Lake Erie north to Lake Simcoe and from Kingston west to the Detroit River. Once the region was a vast hardwood forest. Today the woods of southern Ontario are mostly squared-off woodlots and maple groves, bounded by well-tended fields or country roads.

Early Ontario settlers mostly grew wheat. Today Ontario's farmers may grow corn or canola. They may produce pork, eggs or dairy products, or exotic vegetables to sell to big-city restaurants. On the Niagara Peninsula, they grow grapes for fine Ontario wines.

MUSKOKA COTTAGE COUNTRY

When the farmlands of southern Ontario grew crowded in the late 1800s, settlers tried to farm the land around the Muskoka lakes and Georgian Bay. They soon discovered that the rocky ground there was no place for farmers. Ever since, that region has been known as cottage country: a place to go for hiking, swimming, boating, and camping.

BOREAL FOREST

Most of Ontario, in the vast expanse between the northern Great Lakes and Hudson Bay, is boreal woodland. Spruce and aspen are the most

common trees in the north, while white pine and hard maples are more plentiful closer to the Great Lakes.

The landscape is dotted with tens of thousands of lakes and with fast-flowing whitewater rivers. Some rivers run south to the Great Lakes or the Ottawa River, others flow north to James Bay and Hudson Bay. For thousands of years, until aircraft came to the north, these rivers were the only highways. The northern peoples were master canoe-makers. Fur traders depended on their vessels and their knowledge of the land.

Although the northern forest is thinly populated, it is fiercely argued over. The timber, mineral, and hydroelectric wealth of Ontario lies here, and it attracts logging, mining, and other resource industries to the north. But the northern environment is fragile, and environmentalists demand protection for its irreplaceable wilderness ecology. The Cree and Ojibwa nations, who together call themselves the Anishinabe, still live in and from the northern land, and they vehemently defend their land rights and their way of life.

> Agriculture Canada ranks Canadian farmland into several classes based on quality of soil, growing season, climate conditions, and so on. Most of the first-class farmland found in Canada lies within sight of the CN Tower in Toronto.

NIAGARA ESCARPMENT

The great cliff known as the Niagara Escarpment has been called the spine of southern Ontario. At its southeastern end, it forms the lip over which Niagara Falls plunges. It continues for 725 kilometres, forming "the mountain" at Hamilton, the ski hills of Collingwood, and the spectacular cliffs of the Bruce Peninsula. A hiking trail, the Bruce Trail, follows the escarpment closely, all the way from Niagara Falls to Tobermory, at the tip of the Bruce Peninsula.

1867 Ontario became one of the four founding provinces of Canada. In the time of New France, the area, known then as the upper country, had been held by hunting-gathering Natives in the north and by Native farmers in the south. American refugee Loyalists (colonists who opposed the American Revolution) started a rush of settlers in 1784, and in 1792, Britain founded the colony of Upper Canada. Joined to Lower Canada in 1841, Upper Canada became Ontario at the time of Confederation.

1884 Timothy Eaton, the proprietor of a Toronto department store, introduced the Eaton's catalogue. The next year, the Canadian Pacific Railway began its transcontinental service. Through the catalogue, Eaton's could sell its goods right across the country. The opening of the West helped to keep many Ontario businesses thriving and prospering – often to the annoyance of Westerners, who resented being under the thumb of Eastern businesses.

Timothy Eaton (inset) watches over his first department store.

1910 There were lots of iron foundries around Hamilton, making stoves, tools, and machinery. In 1910, businessmen and financiers joined many of them together to form the Steel Company of Canada, which built a huge new steelmaking enterprise in the city. Stelco (as it was later renamed) and its workers helped make the city into one of the great steelmaking cities of the world.

1912 The Ontario government put an end to French-language education in Ontario schools. Franco-Ontarians fought hard against Regulation 17 (as the ruling was called), and the anti-French prejudice behind it. The government abandoned Regulation 17 in the 1920s, but it was not until 1968 that the right of Franco-Ontarians to learn in their own language was guaranteed.

1937   Oshawa auto workers struck for an eight-hour workday to earn recognition of their union. But Ontario's colourful, hard-hitting premier, Mitch Hepburn, did not want strong unions in Ontario's industries. He formed his own volunteer police, mocked as the "sons of Mitch's," to break the strike. The workers held out, however, and they won all their key demands.

1950S   Canada grew and prospered after the Second World War, and no region did better than southern Ontario. New factories and offices sprouted. So did suburbs, schools, freeways, and shopping centres, particularly in the densely populated Golden Horseshoe, the area around the western end of Lake Ontario.

Premier Mitchell Hepburn (right) shares a laugh with Prime Minister Mackenzie King in 1934.

1965   The newly signed Canada–United States Auto Pact ensured that Canada would build a fair share of the cars and trucks that North Americans drive. Work in Canadian automotive plants and parts plants grew rapidly as a result – and most of the jobs created were in southern Ontario.

1990S   Control of a large share of Canada's economy had helped make Ontario the nation's powerhouse for more than a century. With trade barriers falling all over the world in the 1990s, could Ontario remain as strong and prosperous in a global marketplace?

SIX NATIONS OF GRAND RIVER

They call themselves the Hodenosaunee, "the people of the longhouse." We know them better as the Six Nations, or the Iroquois. In 1784, Thayendanegea (whose English name was Joseph Brant) led those Iroquois who had fought most fiercely against the American Revolution north to a huge tract of land along the Grand River. Even though the government and settlers gradually took away most of the Grand River tract, the Six Nations at Grand River still form the largest single Native community in Canada. There are also several smaller Six Nations reserves in the province.

CREE

The Cree are the people of Ontario's Far North; they live in the boreal forests and the Hudson Bay lowlands. The Cree language has its own alphabet, called Cree syllabics, and today Cree is a written and spoken language. Both the Cree and their more southerly neighbours, the Ojibwa, helped carry the fur trade westwards, and today there are Plains Cree and Plains Ojibwa, as well as those in Ontario. Cree and Ojibwa speak similar Algonquian languages, and together call themselves Anishinabe.

FRANCO-ONTARIANS

Trading and farming families from New France settled around the forts along the lakes of what is now Ontario long before the colony of Upper Canada was founded. Later, francophone immigrants came from Quebec to help build the canals around Welland, to work in the woods and mines of the North, and to clear farms in eastern and northern Ontario. Today half a million Ontarians have French as their mother tongue.

Toronto has been a magnet for immigrants for many decades, and it sometimes claims to be the most multicultural city in the world.

MENNONITES

The Mennonites are followers of Menno Simons, who in the 1500s preached simplicity and peace and told his followers not to serve in anyone's armies. Mennonites began to migrate into Upper Canada from the United States around 1786. Ontario's largest Mennonite community is in Waterloo County, around Kitchener. The most visible Mennonites in this area are the Old Order Mennonites. They dress simply and avoid the use of machinery or electricity. They use horse-drawn ploughs in their fields, and they drive horse-drawn buggies on the local roads.

JAMAICANS

About half a million people from the Caribbean islands live in Canada. About half are Jamaicans (others come from Trinidad, Guyana, Barbados, and smaller countries). Most Jamaican Canadians live in Ontario and have come to Canada since the 1960s, so the community is still young, with many first-generation immigrants and their Canadian-born children. In the early years of Jamaican immigration, many of those who came were young women recruited to work as nannies, often leaving their own families behind for several years.

In cities like Toronto, Jamaicans have contributed many elements from their island culture, including reggae music and popular foods such as jerk chicken. But the community has also struggled with poverty and racism as it works to increase opportunities for young Jamaican Canadians.

Caribbean Canadians celebrate their roots at the annual Caribana parade.

MAPLE GLAZED CAKE

Ontario's multicultural cities offer foods of every part of the world, from Caribbean fish and ackee to fresh mangoes from India. But a favourite treat of all Ontarians is maple syrup, sampled early every spring at sugarbushes and festivals around the province.

3 cups (750 mL) pastry flour
2 1/2 tsp (12 mL) baking powder
1/2 tsp (2 mL) salt
1 cup (250 mL) butter
2 cups (500 mL) granulated sugar
2 tsp (10 mL) maple flavouring
5 eggs
3/4 cup (175 mL) milk
1 cup (250 mL) maple syrup

Grease a 10-inch (25 cm) loaf pan and dust lightly with flour. Sift or blend together flour, baking powder, and salt. Set aside. Cream butter, then blend in sugar and maple flavouring, beating mixture until light and fluffy. Add eggs one at a time, beating well after each one.

Stir dry ingredients into creamed mixture alternately with milk. Turn combined mixture into pan and bake in 350°F (180°C) oven for 60 to 65 minutes or until cake springs back when lightly touched. Cool 5 minutes and remove from pan.

Bring maple syrup to a boil in a small saucepan and simmer to 232°F (110°C) on a candy thermometer. Brush over warm cake and serve.

TORONTO

People outside Toronto sometimes say it thinks it *is* Ontario, or maybe even Canada, and not just a city there. On the other hand, foreign observers sometimes call Toronto "the city that works." They see a clean, lively place with vibrant neighbourhoods, a prosperous city core, preserved architecture, and a tolerance for diversity.

Toronto is Canada's largest city, and it's an important centre of finance, communications, trade, culture, and the arts for the whole country. It got even bigger in 1997, when the government of Ontario merged Toronto and its neighbouring communities into an expanded "megacity."

OTTAWA

When they think of Ottawa, Canadians often think first of the federal government. But the nation's capital is also Ontario's second-largest city. Ottawa began life as a lumber village called Bytown, long before the government arrived in 1865. Today the beautiful Parliament Buildings, standing high above the Ottawa River, along with a network of parks and many unique galleries and museums, make the city an impressive national capital. Yet Ottawa is also one of the coldest national capitals in the world. It celebrates its climate with the Winterlude carnival each February. Every winter, the Rideau Canal, which opened in 1832, turns into an eight-kilometre skating rink winding through the heart of the city.

The construction of the original Parliament Buildings in Ottawa, 1863.

KINGSTON

Close to downtown Kingston stand stone walls adorned with cannons and protected by grassy slopes, tunnels, and ditches. This is Fort Henry, one of a chain of British forts that secured British North America against threats of an American invasion. Kingston is a Loyalist city, founded by American refugees in 1784, and it preserves a handsome architectural legacy from its early settlers. The city is home to Queen's University, the Royal Military College – and several of the country's largest prisons.

STRATFORD

Once Stratford was a railway town in the middle of the Perth County farms. But a local businessman, Tom Patterson, thought a town named for William Shakespeare's birthplace needed a theatre festival. Today the Stratford Shakespeare Festival, which Patterson launched in 1952, is a landmark in Canadian cultural life. It entertains hundreds of thousands of visitors, who come every year for great theatre, fine restaurants, and craft shops – and to picnic in the park, by the peaceful Avon River and its graceful swans.

SUDBURY

When a meteor struck Sudbury 1.82 billion years ago, it left a crater 140 kilometres across and lined with some of the world's richest deposits of nickel and copper. Prospectors who followed the path opened by the Canadian Pacific Railway started Sudbury's mining boom in the 1880s. It has been Ontario's (and Canada's) most important mining town ever since.

Pipers open the Stratford Festival season.

THUNDER BAY

Thunder Bay makes you aware of just how big Ontario is. It sometimes seems a long way from everywhere. But Thunder Bay rarely seems lonely. It's a centre for lake boats, cross-Canada travel, and railway transport, and it has a university, a college, and a lively cultural life. It's also the centre of Finnish Canada, and it keeps alive traditions brought to the North by early immigrants from Finland. Visitors to Thunder Bay discover that many families here enjoy escaping to "camp." The camp is usually a cottage by a quiet lake deep in the woods – and it may be only about fifteen minutes from town.

> Niagara Falls probably started "flowing" only a few thousand years ago. Before then, water from the Great Lakes flowed directly from Lake Huron into the Ottawa River, instead of through Lake Erie and the Niagara River.

NIAGARA FALLS

First there were the falls. Then there were the visitors to the falls. Then there was the tourist trade. For more than a century, Niagara Falls has been home to daredevil stunts, wax museums, honeymoon motels, boat tours under the spray, and every kind of entertainment that visitors will pay to see. Today Niagara Falls has one of Ontario's largest gambling casinos. It also has a butterfly pavilion – a warm, moist indoor jungle, alive with thousands of exotic butterflies. And the falls still roar at the edge of the cliff, though not so loudly now. Much of the Niagara River's flow is diverted underground to drive hydroelectric generators on both sides of the river.

ONTARIO AT WORK

BAY STREET TRADERS

If you want to build a factory, launch your new invention, or open a business, you will probably need money. A stock market is one place to raise the money. Toronto's stock exchange has been the largest and busiest in Canada ever since it started raising money for mines and mills in northern Ontario. Many thousands of Ontarians work for companies that operate the Toronto Stock Exchange, buying and selling shares in ambitious new ventures and established old ones. Bay Street, in downtown Toronto, is the centre of the industry. Canadians often say the words "Bay Street" when they mean big business and wealth, particularly "old" money from central Canada.

FILM CREWS

Dozens of crews make movies and television programs "on location" on Toronto's streets. A fleet of trucks and trailers, and many skilled workers, are needed for every brief shot that is filmed. Toronto is Canada's largest film production centre, although many of the films are not about this country – most films are still made for American markets about American subjects.

AUTO PLANT WORKERS

The automobile industry employs tens of thousands of workers, and Ontario has most of Canada's big automotive plants. Chrysler's big plant is in Windsor, Ford's is in Oakville, and General Motors' is in Oshawa. Asian and European automotive companies also build cars in Ontario. Many manufacturers of automotive parts have plants in the province as well.

Today's assembly lines are cleaner, quieter places than they used to be. The automotive plants are full of robots and computers. But they

Assembly-line workers put the finishing touches on a brand-new car.

still need skilful, highly trained workers who keep up with the latest technologies.

SUDBURY MINERS

These days, you need a college diploma before you get to go down in the mines at Sudbury. Once miners risked their lives to hack minerals from the ground with their pickaxes. Today machines do much of the heavy work. Fewer people go underground, and those who do need specialized skills and extensive training. But mining is still demanding and sometimes dangerous.

OTTAWA LOBBYISTS

Ottawa is the centre of government in Canada, and tens of thousands of civil servants live and work there. Because the government's decisions can affect citizens, businesses, communities, and organizations, Ottawa is also home to many lobbyists and political consultants. Lobbyists promise to keep their clients informed of what the government is doing. They try to influence any government decisions that will affect their employers' interests.

Sixteen-year-old Marilyn Bell heads out for her landmark swim.

MARGARET ATWOOD (1939-   )

She is an internationally famous novelist and poet, and she is well known for supporting nationalist causes. But Margaret Atwood is most often inspired by the city of Toronto, which she has given literary life in novels such as *Life Before Man* and *Cat's Eye*, or by Ontario, the setting of *Surfacing* and the historical novel *Alias Grace*.

MARILYN BELL (1937-   )

She was just a quiet, determined sixteen-year-old in September 1954 when she slipped into the water on the American side of Lake Ontario and started swimming towards Toronto, more than fifty kilometres away. Twenty-one hours later, when she staggered, half-conscious and exhausted, onto a Toronto beach, she was a national hero. Bell went on to set more marathon swim records around the world before retiring to a quiet life.

EDWIN ALONZO BOYD (1914-2002)

A Toronto policeman's son and war veteran, Edwin Boyd became a bank robber "because that's where the money is." Spectacular robberies, and equally spectacular jailbreaks, made his gang famous. Boyd, always dapper and smiling, became a celebrity. But in 1952, two of his gang members killed a police detective. They were later hanged, and Boyd was sentenced to life in prison.

THE DONNELLY FAMILY (D. 1880)

When the Donnelly family emigrated from Ireland to a farm near Lucan, Ontario, they brought all their old family feuds with them. James Donnelly and his big, strong sons were often fighting with their neighbours. On February 4, 1880, an armed gang burst into the Donnelly home. In a few minutes, James, his wife, their two sons, and a niece were all dead. Some of the neighbours were tried in Ontario's most sensational case of murder. But no one was ever convicted.

WAYNE GRETZKY (1961-   )

Who was the greatest hockey player? Most people would say Number 99, Wayne Gretzky from Brantford, Ontario. His father taught him to play when he was only two, and Gretzky just kept getting better. In his first season in the National Hockey League (1979–80), he was the most valuable player and the scoring leader. He went on to break

nearly every NHL record there was, and he led Canadian teams in many world competitions until his retirement in 1999. A great scorer, skater, and passer, he amazed hockey fans above all by his sense of the game.

NED HANLAN (1855–1908)

Ned Hanlan was one of the first professional sports stars and Canada's first world champion solo athlete. His sport was rowing, his trademark a red headband. Rowing was a popular spectator sport in the 1880s, and no one could beat Ned Hanlan. Thousands came out to watch him in the United States, Europe, Australia, and most of all, Canada. When he retired to Toronto, he opened a hotel on the Toronto Islands, where he was born.

JOHN A. MACDONALD (1815–1891)

Sir John A. was not the first to propose Confederation, but he was the most skilful politician among the leaders of the 1860s, and the Confederation deal could not have been struck without him. He was witty and friendly, and he drank too much, but he could always spot where political dangers lay. Those skills made him prime minister in 1867. He was still in office when he died in 1891, watching, he said, "as the gristle of a nation hardened into bone."

NORVAL MORRISSEAU (1932–   )

Life was not easy for Norval Morrisseau. He grew up poor on a northern Ontario reserve. He struggled with alcoholism and was ill at ease among those in the artistic establishment. But in the 1960s, Morrisseau emerged as one of the great Canadian artists. His inspiration came from the beliefs of the Ojibwa mystics and elders. His faith in his cultural heritage and his blazingly colourful paintings inspired a generation of Native Ontario artists.

CATHARINE PARR TRAILL (1802–1899)

Catharine Parr Traill and her husband immigrated to the Peterborough district and settled near her sister, Susanna Moodie, in 1832. Both sisters became well known for the books they wrote about their backwoods existence. But where Susanna was often gloomy and critical, Catharine loved her Canadian experience. She wrote optimistic and helpful books full of detail, including *The Backwoods of Canada.*

Ontario's provincial legislature, Queen's Park, in Toronto.

T he name Ontario is only as old as Confederation. Before 1867 the province was called Canada West, and before 1841 it had been Upper Canada. Its new name came from Lake Ontario. It is usually taken to mean "beautiful lake" in Iroquoian.

Ontario is the only Canadian province where three powerful political parties have competed for decades. During the 1990s, the Liberal Party, the New Democratic Party, and the Progressive Conservative Party all held power for a time. The province began the decade with a Liberal government led by David Peterson of London. A New Democratic government under Bob Rae of Toronto replaced it, only to be replaced in turn by a Progressive Conservative government under Mike Harris from North Bay.

Premier Oliver Mowat fought for provincial rights in the earliest days of Confederation

Ontarians govern themselves through a legislature of 103 members of the provincial Parliament (MPPs). The legislature, in the heart of Toronto, is officially called the Parliament Buildings, but it is known as Queen's Park (after the park that surrounds it). Queen's Park was designed in the Romanesque style by Richard Alfred Waite, and it was built in 1886–93 from reddish-brown sandstone quarried in the Credit River valley, near Toronto. The leader of the party that is supported by the majority of MPPs becomes premier and appoints a Cabinet of ministers to run the government. The lieutenant-governor signs into law bills passed by the legislature.

In the Canadian Parliament in Ottawa, Ontarians are represented by 103 members and six senators. Canada's first prime minister, Sir John A. Macdonald, was an Ontarian from Kingston. Since then, Ontario has provided four more prime ministers – Alexander Mackenzie, Mackenzie Bowell, William Lyon Mackenzie King, and Lester Pearson. Oliver Mowat, who was premier of Ontario from 1871 to 1896, turned himself into one of the first strong provincial leaders of the new Canadian nation. Prime Minister Macdonald had wanted the premiers to do as he told them, but Mowat proved it was not going to be that way in Canada.

JOINED CONFEDERATION:
July 1, 1867

PROVINCIAL MOTTO:
Ut incepit fidelis sic permanet (Loyal it began, loyal it remains)

PROVINCIAL FLOWER:
White trillium

AREA:
1,068,582 square kilometres (10.8 per cent of Canada – Ontario is the second-largest province, after Quebec)

HIGHEST POINT:
Near Temiskaming (693 metres above sea level)

POPULATION:
11,419,046

GROWTH RATE:
6.1 per cent since 1996

CAPITAL:
Toronto

MAIN CITIES:
Toronto (4,682,897 in 2001), Ottawa (774,072), Hamilton (662,401), London (432,451), Windsor (307,827), Oshawa (296,298), Sudbury (155,219), Thunder Bay (121,986)

ONTARIO GOVERNMENT INFORMATION ON THE INTERNET:
www.gov.on.ca

NEVER TRY THIS YOURSELF! THE DAREDEVILS OF NIAGARA

In 1827, while ten thousand people watched, someone sent a schooner loaded with "wild" animals over Niagara Falls. Stunting at the falls was born. It is a "pastime" that has provided some of the most colourful – and the most heart-stopping – moments in the history of Ontario's great tourist attraction.

- In 1859, Blondin, the great French acrobat and the most famous of all the Niagara daredevils, made the first tightrope walk across the falls. Later the same summer, he carried his manager across on his back.
- In 1860, Blondin and the Great Farini (really Bill Hunt) duelled all summer, performing increasingly spectacular tightrope stunts above the falls. Both survived.
- In 1861, the crew of the *Maid of the Mist* took their boat successfully downriver through the Great Gorge and Whirlpool rapids.
- In 1876, Maria Speltrini became the first woman tightrope walker over the falls.
- In 1883, Matthew Webb, who had swum the English Channel, drowned while trying to swim downriver through the Great Gorge rapids.
- In 1901, Annie Taylor, a schoolteacher from Michigan, became the first person to go over Niagara Falls in a barrel. She survived – and said no one should ever do such a thing again.
- In 1911, Lincoln Beachy flew a plane under one of the Niagara bridges.
- In 1920, Charles Stevens became the first daredevil to die trying to go over the falls in a barrel.
- In 1951, Red Hill Jr., who had helped his father, the legendary Red Hill Sr., one of the falls' most famous daredevils, perform twenty-eight life-saving rescues and recover almost two hundred bodies from the Niagara River, died trying to ride the rapids in a barrel.
- In 1960, Roger Woodward, just seven years old, was swept over the falls after a boating accident. He lived – and is to this day the only person to go over the falls unprotected and survive.

MANITOBA

SASKATCHEWAN

LYNN
LAKE

SOUTH
INDIAN
LAKE

THOMPSON

NELSON R

FLIN FLON

THE
PAS

CEDAR
LAKE

NORWAY HOUSE

LAKE
WINNIPEG

LAKE
WINNIPEGOSIS

RIDING
MOUNTAIN
NATIONAL
PARK

ASSINIBOINE RIVER

BRANDON

WINNIPEG

RED RIVE

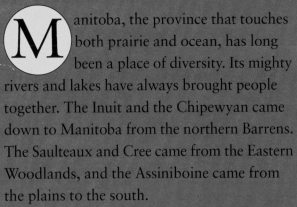

Manitoba, the province that touches both prairie and ocean, has long been a place of diversity. Its mighty rivers and lakes have always brought people together. The Inuit and the Chipewyan came down to Manitoba from the northern Barrens. The Saulteaux and Cree came from the Eastern Woodlands, and the Assiniboine came from the plains to the south.

In the era of the Hudson's Bay Company fur trade, Manitoba was home to French and English traders and voyageurs. The Métis people, with their blended Native and European ancestry, emerged here. In 1869–70, as the Hudson's Bay Company prepared to give its authority over Manitoba to the new Canadian nation, the Métis took up arms to ensure that they would join the Confederation on their own terms.

Then the transcontinental railway put Winnipeg at the centre of the continent, and Manitoba found its modern place as a Canadian crossroads. With the new province established, immigrants came first from Ontario, later from Europe, and more recently from many parts of the world. Early settlers came to farm the fertile flatlands of the Red River. Later arrivals headed for the forests and the mines of the north.

Today Manitoba remains among the most ethnically diverse of Canadian provinces. It is home to citizens who boast German, Ukrainian, Mennonite, French, Métis, Jewish, British, and Native Canadian roots, among many others.

Geography divides Manitoba in two. The northern and eastern two-thirds of the province form a rugged northern environment. This part of Manitoba stands on some of the world's oldest rock, the Canadian Shield, a broad, flat plate of the earth's crust that is about six hundred million years old. Much of the Shield country of northern Manitoba is rich in forest resources and minerals. Fast-flowing rivers cut through the rock on their way down to Hudson Bay. The lowlands they cross near the shore, however, are very different: they are a flat, treeless expanse prowled by polar bears that come inland from the sea ice.

Manitoba's other geographic region, the southwestern third of the province, is flat or rolling open country. Once it was grassland interspersed with glades of forest, home to buffalo and antelope and the peoples who hunted them. Today its richly fertile soil is the best farming land anywhere in the West. This is the densely settled part of Manitoba, and the area where most of its cities stand.

Majestic Lake Winnipeg.

MANITOBA LAKES AND RIVERS

Lake Winnipeg, Lake Manitoba, and Lake Winnipegosis are remnants of glacial Lake Agassiz. They rank among Canada's largest lakes, not counting the five Great Lakes. Lake Winnipeg, which once was home to transport ships and sternwheelers, still supports a commercial fishing fleet. The fishing fleet brings in a Manitoba delicacy: Winnipeg goldeye, a small herring-like fish found in these waters.

THE LAKE AGASSIZ BASIN AND THE RED RIVER VALLEY

Rivers flow into the lowlands of southern Manitoba from the east, the south, and the west. About twelve thousand years ago, towards the end of the last ice age, an inland sea covered most of Manitoba. Scientists call it Lake Agassiz, and it was many times larger than today's Lake Superior.

The waters of Lake Agassiz gradually drained away, and one legacy they left is the rich farmland of southern Manitoba. Sediments laid down at the bottom of Lake Agassiz covered the bedrock and produced the remarkably flat terrain through which rivers like the Red now flow.

Lake Agassiz has brought prosperity to Manitoba farmers, but it has also brought deadly floods when the rivers overflow their beds and spread across the flat Agassiz plain. Deep snow and a sudden thaw in the American headwaters of the Red River can bring disaster to the Manitobans living downriver.

NORTHERN FORESTS

A large portion of Manitoba is Shield country, a landscape of ancient rocks where much of the original topsoil was scoured away and carried south by glaciers. But there are rich resources to be found in the Shield. Forests of spruce, pine, aspen, and birch cover the ground. The rock itself is rich in mineral resources, and Manitoba's wild rivers generate most of the hydroelectric power of the three Prairie provinces. Northern Manitoba is scattered with resource towns, each built around a lumber mill, a mine, or a power dam. Manitoba has always also been home to Native communities dedicated to fishing, trapping, and hunting.

Louis Riel (centre) and the Provisional Government, 1869.

1870 Manitoba was the only place where violence marked the path to provincehood within Confederation. The founders of Canada had always intended for the new nation to expand westwards, and in 1868, the government began negotiating to take over the interests of the Hudson's Bay Company and Britain in the northwest. But little attention was paid to the people living at Red River. The Red River settlers formed what they called the Provisional Government, led by Louis Riel, to protect their interests and negotiate with Canada. This might have been a mostly peaceful negotiation. There had been conflicts within the Red River settlement, however, and the provisional government had jailed many of its opponents and even executed one of them, Thomas Scott. The Canadian government sent troops to reimpose order, and Louis Riel, instead of being hailed as the founder of a new province, had to flee into exile as the troops approached.

1872 The Canadian government began offering land to "homesteaders." Anyone who could clear land and build a house would receive 160 acres (about 66 hectares) almost for free. Attracted by this offer, settlers began to flow in from crowded Ontario and Quebec, the United States, and eventually eastern Europe as well. Soon the Métis and French-speaking Manitobans were a small minority, and the provincial government abolished the language guarantees that had been given to them in 1870.

1881 "The bustle and stir can only compare to Wall Street, New York," a visitor said about Winnipeg in 1881. The Canadian Pacific Railway was beginning to move, and Winnipeg was at the heart of the action. The new city was growing like wildfire, and anyone who owned a piece of land could expect to be rich.

1897 Settlers from central and eastern Europe began to arrive in Manitoba. When they sent back word about *vilni zemli* – "free land," in Ukrainian – a flood of immigrants began to pour across the ocean, along the railway, and into the province.

1919 Times were bad for working people in Winnipeg, and they organized to do something about it. In May, trade unionists called a general strike. To back their demand for better wages and working conditions, they closed down factories and stores, as well as transit lines and public services. It was the biggest strike ever seen in Canada. Even the police, firefighters, and the telephone company took part. Owners and managers of companies fought the strike, and volunteer strikebreakers tried to keep city services going. The government supported them. Amid riots and arrests, the strike was smashed and its leaders jailed or deported.

1927 A big copper-and-zinc mine and refinery opened in Flin Flon, a first step in exploiting Manitoba's rich mineral resources.

1950 One of the worst Red River floods drove more than one hundred thousand people from their homes in Winnipeg and the surrounding area and flooded out fifteen thousand buildings.

1968 Manitoba completed the Red River Floodway and Greater Winnipeg Diversion. It was designed to carry floodwaters past the city and prevent disastrous floods like those of 1950. But it was a huge and very expensive project. And could the Red River floods be controlled? When the diversion was done, Manitobans began waiting for the great flood that would test it.

1972 A new mining town, Lynn Lake, arose in northern Manitoba, and this one was something special. The government, not the mining company, built the town, and it wanted to make Lynn Lake a model example of a town designed for northern living. Lynn Lake was built around a unique town centre. All its services, schools, and businesses were clustered together so that its people could move around in warmth and comfort, sheltered from the snow and cold of winter.

1997 The so-called Hundred Year Flood was the greatest rising of the Red River in more than a century. In the open country south of Winnipeg, thousands of farms and some small towns were flooded. Many rural Manitobans were driven from their homes, and the Canadian army moved in to help with the clean-up. But around Winnipeg, the floodways and diversions worked well. The city was saved from devastation.

A Saulteaux Native travelling with his family near Lake Winnipeg, about 1825.

SAULTEAUX

Saulteaux is a French word meaning "people of the falls." The Saulteaux people had once lived around the falls at Sault Ste. Marie in Ontario, but they migrated west in the early days of the fur trade and became people of the plains around Winnipeg.

MÉTIS

Métis means "mixed." The Métis are the descendants of a mixing of people who were first brought together by the fur trade: particularly Ojibwa, Cree, French, English, and Scots. Gradually, as Métis migrated from fur-trade forts to the prairie, they developed their own language, called Michif, and their own distinctive culture and customs. The Red River valley was the centre of Métis life in the 1870s. Although many Métis moved farther west, following the buffalo and retreating from encroaching settlers, their traditions remain strong in Manitoba.

MENNONITES

Communities of German and Swiss Mennonites from the United States settled in Ontario in the 1780s. A hundred years later, it was Russian Mennonites who formed a new Mennonite community in Manitoba. In the 1920s and after the Second World War, more Mennonite refugees joined them from eastern Europe, making Manitoba the centre of Mennonite life in Canada.

Mennonites have traditionally lived in communities that preserve the German language; they have tried to keep separate from the rest of the world and to take care of their own needs as much as possible. Today, however, Mennonites are an important part of Manitoba society, and many have become prominent in the arts, business, and politics.

ICELANDERS

In the 1870s, hard times forced Icelanders to think of leaving their home island in the North Atlantic to settle elsewhere. In 1875, the first

Icelanders came to Manitoba, where they established the farming and fishing community they called New Iceland. Small groups of Icelanders continued to migrate, either directly from Iceland or by way of the United States, and a thriving Icelandic community grew up around Gimli. Some of the greatest poets and writers of Icelandic literature grew up in Manitoba's Icelandic community. Every year, Gimli holds its Icelandic festival, the Islendingadagurinn.

FRANCO-MANITOBANS

Explorers from New France built trading posts in Manitoba as early as the 1730s, when Pierre de La Vérendrye hoped the Saskatchewan River would lead him to the Western Sea (the Pacific Ocean). Later, in the 1800s, the French-speaking Métis dominated the Red River community, and their leaders and priests built strong ties between French Manitoba and Quebec. After Confederation, Quebeckers were among the Eastern migrants pouring into the new province of Manitoba. French-speakers soon became a small minority there, but many of their language rights were abolished. In the 1980s and 1990s, Franco-Manitobans, though still a minority, began to recover the rights that had been taken away in the 1890s.

POACHED WINNIPEG GOLDEYE

The Winnipeg goldeye is a small silvery fish found in the Winnipeg, Red, and Assiniboine rivers. It becomes one of Manitoba's favourite delicacies when it's carefully smoked over a fire of willow wood. An easier method of preparing the fish, while still retaining its delicate flavour, is to poach it in water.

1 goldeye per serving

Place goldeye (with head and tail on or off, as desired) on a piece of greased foil. Fold foil over fish, securing open edges with double folds to make watertight.

Place package in a pot of rapidly boiling water. When water returns to a boil, cover and cook for 10 minutes (20 minutes if fish is frozen). Serve hot, with lemon wedges.

Unwrapped goldeye may be cooked for 15 to 20 minutes in a steamer as an alternative.

Downtown Winnipeg, 1882.

WINNIPEG

Often challenged but never replaced, Winnipeg remains the gateway to the Canadian West. It is home to half of all Manitobans; in no other province does one city loom so large. In 1972, when it absorbed several cities and towns around it into a "unicity," Winnipeg became Canada's largest major city in area. It is a centre of government, industry, transportation, and culture. It has produced writers, politicians, and the internationally renowned dancers of the Royal Winnipeg Ballet. Once Winnipeg's leaders tried hard to keep their city "British," and they worried about foreign immigrants. Today Winnipeg celebrates its diversity.

ST-BONIFACE

St-Boniface, just across the Red River from Winnipeg, is one of the larger francophone communities in Canada outside Quebec. It began as a Catholic mission church in 1818, and though it is now part of the city of Winnipeg, it remains the heart of Franco-Manitoban life in the province. St-Boniface has French-language radio, television, and newspapers; a cultural centre; and the yearly Festival du Voyageur.

FLIN FLON

In a cabin in the north of Manitoba, a prospector came across an abandoned novel that featured an eccentric character named Josiah Flintabbatey Flonatin. When rich zinc and copper resources were discovered nearby and a new mining town began to spring up, the fictional character inspired a name. Founded in 1927, Flin Flon has been a mining and smelting centre ever since, and it is famous for producing hockey stars too.

STEINBACH

In 1874, Mennonite pioneers founded a communal settlement fifty kilometres southeast of Winnipeg. Steinbach is "hometown central" to many thousands of Mennonite Manitobans from the prosperous agricultural region around the town. Steinbach's Mennonite Village Museum is a reconstruction of the original settlement of the Mennonite pioneers.

> **Portage and Main, the intersection of downtown Winnipeg, was a junction of Native trails for hundreds, or thousands, of years before the city was built.**

YORK FACTORY

York Factory, on Hudson Bay at the mouth of the Hayes River, is said to be the oldest permanently settled community in Manitoba. It was founded in 1684 by the Hudson's Bay Company. (In those days, a "factory" was another name for a trading post.) York Factory controlled the company's trade with the whole Saskatchewan River system far to the west. It also gave its name to the York boat, a large, shallow

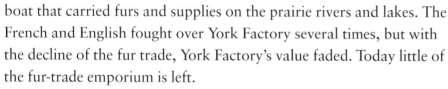

boat that carried furs and supplies on the prairie rivers and lakes. The French and English fought over York Factory several times, but with the decline of the fur trade, York Factory's value faded. Today little of the fur-trade emporium is left.

CHURCHILL

Fur traders came to the mouth of the Churchill River later than they did to York Factory (which is farther down the coast of Hudson Bay), and they came only to tap the far northern trade of the Chipewyan peoples. But to defend the harbour from French rivals, the Hudson's Bay Company built Fort Prince of Wales, a remarkable stone bastion that is now a spectacular abandoned ruin.

Churchill survived the end of the fur trade because of its deepwater port and the railway that links it to southern Manitoba. (Churchill is actually closer by sea to Europe than Montreal is.) During the 1950s, Churchill became been a centre of rocket research. Today tourists come to see the scores of polar bears that congregate on the shores in the fall.

RIDING MOUNTAIN

On a high escarpment above the prairie, Riding Mountain National Park is a unique mix of boreal forest, grasslands, streams, and bog, and it's home to a rich diversity of animal and plant life. The national park, established in 1929, is a popular attraction for hikers, cross-country skiers, and campers.

Riding Mountain National Park.

MANITOBA AT WORK

GRAIN EXCHANGE TRADERS

What will the price of wheat be next fall? If anyone knows the answer, it is the traders on the floor of the Winnipeg Commodity Exchange, where everyone involved in buying and selling grain meets to deal in actual and future crops. The farmers may grow the grain, but it is the traders who match up buyers and sellers – and decide what price the farmers will get for their crops.

The Commodity Exchange began as the Grain Exchange in 1887, soon after the railway started shipping prairie grain out through Winnipeg. It continues to be the main farm-related commodities exchange in Canada, though it also deals in other products now. As long as grain-growing is big business on the Prairies, Winnipeg expects its exchange to be the place where the crop is bought and sold each year.

> A hundred years ago, workers from Atlantic Canada and Ontario would travel to Manitoba every fall on "harvest excursion" trains to help bring in the harvest.

POLAR BEAR TOUR OPERATORS

Want to see polar bears, lots of polar bears? Churchill, Manitoba, is the place people come to from all over the world. For most of the year, the big white bears are solitary creatures that roam the inaccessible sea ice alone. But along the Hudson Bay lowlands, the bears come in to the tundra in summer. In fall, they congregate along the shore, waiting for the ice to form again on the bay. From Churchill, well-protected buses on high wheels take visitors out for close – but safe – encounters with polar bears.

Curious polar bears in Churchill.

MENNONITE RELIEF WORKERS

You might meet Manitoba Mennonites digging a well in West Africa or helping to build schools in Latin America. Private and personal charity work – instead of government aid – has always been part of the Mennonite creed. The Mennonite Central Committee, based in Winnipeg, spends millions of dollars every year supporting self-help, economic development, and peace in developing countries, and many young Mennonites have gone overseas in support of that cause.

BUSH PILOTS

You can't get there from here – except by plane. In the 1920s and 1930s, aviation changed travel around northern Manitoba forever. Suddenly, isolated trappers and prospectors could get supplies, medical help, or a ride back to Winnipeg anytime they needed. Soon, several bush pilots had achieved a kind of folk-hero status. James Richardson, a Winnipeg grain dealer, founded Western Canadian Airways in 1926. Punch Dickins, a First World War fighter pilot from Portage la Prairie, joined him in 1927, eventually becoming one of the greatest Canadian bush pilots. Dickins flew the first prairie airmail routes and led aerial mapping surveys of much of the province.

Grey Owl and a baby beaver.

GREY OWL (1888-1938)

Grey Owl was a hero and a fraud at the same time. Archie Belaney of England came to Canada as a teenager and worked as a trapper. His Iroquois wife, Anahareo, taught him to love and protect wildlife, and soon he claimed he was Grey Owl, a Native expert on northern nature and wildlife. As Grey Owl, Archie Belaney became the most popular Native Canadian in the world, writing books and lecturing widely on the need to protect and conserve the wilderness. Grey Owl had several different homes in the forests of northern Canada, but some of his most important writing was about the beavers of Riding Mountain in Manitoba. His secret identity was revealed only after he died.

MARGARET LAURENCE (1926-1987)

The writer Margaret Laurence lived in Africa, Britain, Vancouver, and Ontario, but her finest work was inspired by her Manitoba hometown of Neepawa. She remade it into the fictional town of Manawaka, and in her novels and stories, Manawaka became one of the great places of Canadian literature. *The Diviners*, her last great novel, combines the stories of Scots and Métis Manitobans into a universal experience.

JOHN NORQUAY (1841-1889)

John Norquay's Métis family were fur traders and farmers, and young John was a good student in the Red River schools. He went into politics when Manitoba became a province, and he served as premier from 1878 until 1887. During the fast-changing era of railways and settlers, Norquay was a popular representative of the Métis, Franco-Manitobans, and long-established "old settlers" of the Red River. He is the only Métis ever to have been premier of Manitoba.

PEGUIS (ABOUT 1774-1864)

Peguis was born among the Saulteaux people near Sault Ste. Marie. He moved to the Red River valley as the fur-trading Saulteaux relocated from the lakes towards the prairies. In 1812, when the Hudson's Bay Company brought a group of colonists, the Red River settlers, to Manitoba, Peguis was chief of the Saulteaux, and he helped the suffering immigrants in their early years. He and Lord Selkirk, the founder of the Red River Colony, made a treaty in 1817. Later, Peguis regretted that the settlers had not lived up to their promises to his people.

FAMOUS AND INFAMOUS

LOUIS RIEL (1844-1885)

Hanged as a traitor in Saskatchewan, Louis Riel has also been hailed as the greatest of Manitobans. He remains one of the most controversial figures of Canadian history. In 1870, he was the best-educated and most well travelled young Métis of Manitoba, and his people made him leader of the provisional government of Red River. Riel led the Métis community as it stood up to the government of Canada for the rights of the people of the prairies. He fled into exile in 1870, but Manitobans showed their continued support by electing him to the Canadian House of Commons several times.

In later years, Riel began to believe he was the saviour of the Métis people and the prophet of a new religion. In 1884, Métis hunters and farmers who had settled in Saskatchewan were angry to see settlers and the Canadian government once more invading their community. They invited Riel back to lead them, and he spearheaded the brief, unsuccessful North-West Rebellion of 1885, for which he was executed at Regina. Riel was buried at St-Boniface. He remains a hero to many Métis, Westerners, and francophone Canadians.

GABRIELLE ROY (1909-1983)

Born in St-Boniface, Gabrielle Roy began working as a teacher there before becoming a writer. Much of her writing was done in Montreal, the setting of her first, and most famous, novel, *The Tin Flute*. This book established her as one of the great French-language writers of her time, but she never forgot her Manitoba home. Always inspired by the Western landscape and its mixture of cultures, she set several of her books in Manitoba, including *Where Nests the Water Hen*.

VILHJALMUR STEFANSSON (1879-1962)

Born in an Icelandic community at Arnes, Manitoba, Vilhjalmur Stefansson soon moved with his family to the United States. After studying anthropology at Harvard University, he returned to Canada to become an explorer of the Arctic. From 1913 to 1918, he was one of the leaders of a Canadian expedition to the Arctic islands, and he identified and mapped some of the world's last undiscovered landmasses there. In his most famous book, *The Friendly Arctic*, he argued that the North was not a wasteland but a valuable and habitable region ripe for development.

Manitoba's Beaux Arts legislature.

As a place name, Manitoba is only as old as the province, which joined Confederation under that name (suggested to the Canadian government by Louis Riel) in 1870. The Hudson's Bay Company had considered what is now Manitoba part of its trading territory, called Rupert's Land. Many of the settlers of the Red River valley simply called their community Red River.

At first, the province of Manitoba was only a small area around Winnipeg, but it expanded its boundaries several times before achieving its modern shape in 1912. The word *manitoba*, which had been given first to the lake and then to the province, comes from an Algonquian word meaning "mystery" or "mysterious being."

Manitoba has been governed by Native nations, by the law of the

Hudson's Bay Company, by Métis custom, and (as a province of Canada) by legal codes borrowed both from Quebec and Ontario.

The people of Manitoba elect a legislature of fifty-seven men and women, known as members of the Legislative Assembly (MLAs). The party supported by a majority of MLAs forms a government, which "advises" the lieutenant-governor, who is the ceremonial head of the provincial administration. In Ottawa, Manitoba is represented by fourteen members of Parliament and six senators.

The Manitoba legislative building in Winnipeg was designed in the Beaux Arts style by the British architect Frank W. Simon and built from limestone from the quarries of Tyndall between 1912 and 1920 (although it was not officially opened until 1929). Its most famous feature is Charles Gardet's sculpture, which sits on top of its tall dome. This is the *Golden Boy*, a statue of a Greek runner carrying a torch and a sheaf of wheat. He faces north, where the future of the province was believed to lie.

No Manitoban has been prime minister of Canada. But one Manitoban with great influence in national politics was James Shaver Woodsworth (1874–1942). A Methodist minister who ran a mission in Winnipeg's North End, Woodsworth became a pacifist and a socialist. He was arrested for supporting the strikers during the Winnipeg General Strike of 1919, and North End voters elected him to the Canadian House of Commons in 1921. In 1933, he was chosen leader of the Co-operative Commonwealth Federation (CCF), which became the New Democratic Party (NDP) in 1961. Woodsworth inspired much of the tradition of socialist and social-democratic parliamentary parties in twentieth-century Canada.

J. S. Woodsworth launched his political career during the Winnipeg General Strike.

The example set by Woodsworth was carried on by Stanley Knowles (1908–1997), another Manitoban CCF and NDP member of Parliament. Knowles was one of Canada's greatest parliamentarians. When he retired from active politics, the House of Commons made him an officer of the House so he could remain as an adviser to the Parliament he loved.

JOINED CONFEDERATION:
July 15, 1870

PROVINCIAL MOTTO:
Manitoba has no provincial motto

PROVINCIAL FLOWER:
Prairie crocus

AREA:
650,000 square kilometres

HIGHEST POINT:
Baldy Mountain (832 metres above sea level)

POPULATION:
1,119,583

GROWTH RATE:
Down 0.5 per cent since 1996

CAPITAL:
Winnipeg

MAIN CITIES:
Winnipeg (671,274 in 2001), Brandon (45,037), Thompson (13,256),
Portage la Prairie (20,617)

**MANITOBA GOVERNMENT INFORMATION ON THE
INTERNET:**
www.gov.mb.ca

THE WINNIPEG GENERAL STRIKE

Winnipeg was a working-class town in 1919. Railway yards and factories employed thousands, and many of the workers were immigrants. Some had come from Britain, some from eastern Europe.

In 1919, the workers of Winnipeg were angry. The First World War was over, but many people were unemployed. Prices were shooting up, but the workers' wages did not rise. The working day was long, and conditions were often harsh and dangerous.

In those days, labour unions had few rights in Canada, but working people were desperate for change. They began to organize. "One big union" – all workers joined together – was a favourite cry. The idea spread to many Canadian cities, but Winnipeggers were particularly ready to listen and to act.

In May 1919, Winnipeg's building contractors refused to give a raise to their labourers. The call went out for a strike – and not just by the workers in the building trades, but by all workers in the city. In a few hours, thirty thousand men and women had walked off jobs throughout Winnipeg. Factories stopped. The trains stopped. Stores closed. Police officers, firefighters, and postal workers offered to join the strike.

The strikers promised that they would continue to provide all the vital services the city urgently needed. But leaders of business and industry feared worker power. They wanted to break the strikers, not negotiate with them. The employers, the city government, and the federal government in Ottawa all worked together to smash the strike. City leaders called the strikers troublemakers. They had them thrown in jail. Strike leaders who were immigrants were shipped out of Canada.

On "Bloody Saturday," June 17, the police were ordered to break up a march of strikers. Officers on horseback rode into crowds of workers in downtown Winnipeg. Angry strikers turned over streetcars and set them alight. Fights raged through the streets. One striker was killed. Soon the army took charge of the city, and the government demanded that the strikers give up their demands.

The pressure on the workers was too much to bear. At the end of June 1919, after more than a month, Winnipeg's "general strike" collapsed. The strikers had to go back to work. It would be twenty-five years before Canadian workers were guaranteed the right to form unions for collective bargaining.

SASKATCHEWAN

ALBERTA

URANIUM CITY

LAKE
ATHABASCA

FOND-DU-LAC

WOLLASTON
LAKE

CREE
LAKE

REINDEER
LAKE

LAC
LA
RONGE

LA RONGE

NORTH SASKATCHEWAN RIVER

PRINCE ALBERT

NORTH
BATTLEFORD

DUCK
LAKE

MELFORT

BATTLEFORD

BATOCHE

SASKATOON

HUMBOLDT

SOUTH SASKATCHEWAN RIVER

YORK

ESTERHA

INDIAN
HEAD

QU'APPELLE R

SWIFT
CURRENT

MOOSE
JAW

REGINA

CYPRESS
HILLS

GRAVELBOURG

WEYBURN

STOUGH

PALLISER'S TRIANGLE

ESTEVAN

MANITOBA

First of all, Saskatchewan is not as flat as people think. The province actually slopes from west to east – which is why its rivers flow in from Alberta and out to Manitoba. In addition, much of the prairie and the wooded "parkland" is gently rolling and broken by coulees (ravines) and sheltered river valleys. The Cypress Hills, in the southwestern corner of the province, are the highest ground between the Rockies and Labrador.

But Saskatchewan *is* dry. Most of it gets more sunshine and less rainfall than any other province. The open prairie is one of the great wheat-growing regions of the world – but the fields of golden grain prosper only if they receive enough moisture during the long, hot days of a prairie summer.

When immigrant farmers poured into Saskatchewan a hundred years ago, they hoped that wealth and security were just around the corner. Their new home turned out to be tougher than that. Droughts, dust bowls, and crop failures have hammered the prairies, and the decisions of distant governments and wheat buyers could be just as destructive. Saskatchewan's people learned to trust their own resources and to help each other, and the province helped launch the "co-op" movement, medicare, and other initiatives.

As Canada's breadbasket, Saskatchewan is a farmers' province, but it also has important mineral resources in uranium and potash. Another Saskatchewan resource is its people. Because modern farming produces more food with fewer people, Saskatchewan has "exported" many brilliant citizens to other provinces, where they have succeeded in many walks of life. For those at home, the struggle to maintain lively cities, successful family farms, and a vibrant society goes on.

LANDSCAPES

"There's not a whole lot, but there's lots of it." This is how Saskatchewan farmers describe the landscape that defines them – lots of land for farming and grazing, lots of blue sky arching over the horizons. Gently rolling more often than flat, and cut deeply by river valleys that shelter trees and animals, Saskatchewan was shaped by retreating glaciers that left behind the rich grasslands that became the best wheat-growing acreage in the world. The province, in fact, has almost half of all the arable land in Canada.

THE QU'APPELLE VALLEY

Sheltered and tree-lined, this broad valley carries the Qu'Appelle River through a series of lakes and parks towards Manitoba. The valley floor is rich farmland, and the north slopes are famous for their crops of berries, including the Saskatoon berry, a local favourite. It is said that the name comes from a young man who thought he heard his faraway lover calling. "*Qu'appelle?*" he replied, "Who calls?" But he heard only his own voice echoing back across the valley. His sweetheart was dead.

Fall in the Qu'Appelle Valley.

MR. PALLISER'S DRY TRIANGLE

Could farmers thrive in the land between the hot American desert and the cold northern tundra of the West? In the 1850s, the British government sent an Irish adventurer, John Palliser, to find out. For three years, Palliser and his scientists travelled the prairie. They identified a rich fertile belt along

the North Saskatchewan River, but they decided that what they called Palliser's Triangle, the area along the American border, was too dry for farming. Homesteaders began to farm and ranch in Palliser's Triangle during the unusually rainy 1880s, however, and the government encouraged them. Many of the settlers of the Triangle were driven out in the dry decades that followed.

WASCANA LAKE

When the place called Pile o' Bones was renamed Regina in 1883, it was little more than a railway station on the bald prairie. Since then, the people of Regina have transformed their landscape. They began by planting trees and damming Wascana Creek to create Wascana Lake and Wascana Park. Today the scenic waterway winds through the heart of the tree-shaded city.

The park is home to Saskatchewan's legislature, the University of Regina, and the Saskatchewan Centre for the Arts.

CYPRESS HILLS

From fourteen hundred metres above sea level, Saskatchewan does not look flat. The Cypress Hills were named for the forests of pine – *cyprès*, in Métis French – that cover the slopes of this mountainous southwestern corner of the province. The hills were the only part of the province not buried by glaciers in the ice ages of twenty thousand years ago. They were a refuge from which plants and animals repopulated the prairies as the ice retreated.

MOMENTS

A North-West Mounted Police encampment in the Cypress Hills, 1879.

1870 When Canada acquired land in the North and the from Britain and the Hudson's Bay Company, what is today Saskatchewan became part of the North-West Territories.

1874 Officers from the newly founded North-West Mounted Police were ordered to quell the troubles between hunters and smugglers who were invading Native encampments in the Cypress Hills. To get there, the Mounties made a long march across the drylands of southern Saskatchewan.

1882 The Saskatchewan and Assiniboia districts of the North-West Territories were established. Assiniboia's capital was at Pile o' Bones, soon to be Regina, and the capital of the Saskatchewan district was Battleford, on the North Saskatchewan River, where the Mounties made their headquarters.

1885 Led by Louis Riel and Gabriel Dumont, the Métis people of Saskatchewan rose in rebellion against encroaching settlers and the neglectful Canadian government. Troops sent out on the newly built Canadian Pacific Railway crushed the rebellion at Batoche.

1905 Canada finally agreed to make provinces of the prairie sections of the North-West Territories. Should there be one big province? If there were to be two provinces, should the boundary between them run north-south or east-west? Local wishes were not much considered when Ottawa created Alberta and Saskatchewan and gave them the boundaries they have today.

1907 Canadian scientists looking for varieties of wheat that would be better suited to prairie conditions sent a few bags of a new seed to the experimental station at Indian Head, Saskatchewan. It prospered. The new kind of wheat, called Marquis, took the prairies by storm and made the Canadian West into the breadbasket of the world.

1912 On June 30, a cyclone destroyed scores of buildings and killed twenty-eight people in Regina.

1924 Wheat farmers founded the Saskatchewan Wheat Pool

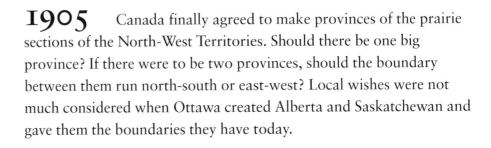

to market their grain. The wheat pool became one of Canada's largest corporations, and it is still owned by Prairie farmers.

1929   When the Great Depression struck the world, the price of wheat plunged. At the same time, a terrible eight-year drought began to lash the southern Prairies. The darkest period of Saskatchewan's history had begun.

1931   The provincial population was 921,000, but farmers were being driven out by the drought and the Depression. It would be almost fifty years before the population reached one million.

The Great Depression brought poverty to families all over the Prairies.

1933   A new political party, the Co-operative Commonwealth Federation (CCF), held a meeting in Regina in 1933, during the worst of the Depression. From that meeting emerged the Regina Manifesto, which called for public ownership of industry and promised pensions, health and welfare insurance, unemployment insurance, and other programs to help ordinary Canadians through hard times. The Regina Manifesto influenced Canadian politics for the next fifty years.

1944   Saskatchewan elected North America's first socialist government. The CCF government, led by Premier Tommy Douglas until 1961, remained in power for twenty years.

1951   Systematic exploration for Saskatchewan potash began. Pioneers used to make potash, a potassium-rich mineral useful for fertilizer, from wood ashes, but in a few places around the world, the mineral can be mined from deep underground deposits.

1962   Saskatchewan's New Democratic government introduced North America's first medicare program, providing full medical care for all citizens, whether rich or poor. The province's plan soon became the model for all of Canada.

1981   Saskatchewan's population was just over one million, but it was about to begin declining again.

1996   Saskatchewan's population was 990,000.

WOODLAND HUNTERS

Not all of Saskatchewan is prairie grassland. Where the subarctic forests of northern Canada cross the northern third of Saskatchewan, Athabaskan-speaking peoples have always hunted moose and woodland caribou and harvested fish and wild rice from the northern waters. Northern Saskatchewan is also rich in beaver – one fur trader called the Athabaska country "the fur traders' Eldorado."

The Plains Cree chief Big Bear (standing, centre) encouraged his people to trade with and adapt to the new settlers when the railway came and the buffalo were killed off.

PEOPLE OF THE BUFFALO

The grasslands that today produce wheat and canola were once home to millions of buffalo. The Plains people, including the Cree, the Ojibwa, the Assiniboine, and the Gros Ventre, hunted the buffalo on foot, trapping their prey in pens called buffalo pounds or driving them over cliffs at buffalo jumps.

The coming of guns and horses in the 1700s changed the life of the Plains hunters dramatically. Both hunting and travel became easier, and the brightest period of prairie Native culture began. But woodland bands and Métis hunters also came to the plains, and sports hunters soon followed. No one could believe that the vast herds of buffalo could be thinned out. But the population simply collapsed during the 1870s, and the last wild herds were hunted out in the 1880s. Leaders of the hunting peoples tried desperately to shift their people to farming, with little success.

The Métis leader Gabriel Dumont in the 1880s.

UKRAINIANS

Ukrainians came to Canada in the hundreds of thousands from the 1890s to the 1950s, and they settled all across the Prairies and in many other parts of Canada. But the sight of an onion-shaped Orthodox church rising above a Saskatchewan wheat field symbolizes the huge contribution they made to Saskatchewan. "Men in sheepskin coats," a Canadian politician once called them. At first they were farmers and labourers. Today they contribute to every aspect of Saskatchewan society. Now that Ukraine is an independent nation, some young Ukrainian Canadians have even gone "home" to help lead the struggling new nation to prosperity.

REMITTANCE MEN

It's one of those Saskatchewan legends – the black-sheep son of some proper English gentry family is sent out to the colonies with a monthly "remittance" of cash, just so long as he never comes home. Why they would all have come to Saskatchewan, no one can say, but the name and the idea were common in the province for generations.

SASKATOON BERRY AND RHUBARB JAM

Saskatchewan has been the breadbasket of the nation for a hundred years, so any dish with bread or wheat is good Saskatchewan fare. But one of the foods most associated with the province is the sweet purple saskatoon berry. Early settlers depended heavily on these berries, which were sometimes the only fruit they got. Today they are still a favourite, and they work well with the rhubarb in this unforgettable jam.

6 cups (1.5 L) saskatoon berries
4 cups (1 L) diced rhubarb
1/2 cup (125 mL) water
6 cups (1.5 L) sugar

Wash, stem, and mash saskatoon berries. Set aside. Wash and dice rhubarb, then combine in a saucepan with water. Bring to a boil and simmer, covered, until soft (about 5 minutes). Stir in saskatoon berries and bring mixture back to a boil.

Next, slowly stir sugar into hot fruit. Bring mixture to a boil once again and let boil, uncovered, for about 10 minutes. Stir frequently.

Spoon mixture into sterilized jars and seal tightly while hot to prevent spoilage. Makes about 8 to 10 jars.

The City of Bridges on the South Saskatchewan River.

SASKATOON

Regina is the capital of Saskatchewan, but Saskatoon is actually slightly larger in population. It was founded in 1882 by a community of settlers committed to temperance (that is, refraining from alcoholic drink). They named the new town for the bright red berry that grows locally, and it began to prosper as railways arrived. Today Saskatoon is the home of the University of Saskatchewan and a centre for the nearby potash mines and the northern uranium industry. Seven bridges span the picturesque South Saskatchewan River as it flows through the city.

PRINCE ALBERT

Named for Queen Victoria's husband, the town of Prince Albert, on the North Saskatchewan River, stands almost exactly at the centre of the province. It has the distinction of having been represented in Canada's Parliament by three prime ministers. John Diefenbaker lived in Prince Albert, and Wilfrid Laurier of Quebec and William Lyon Mackenzie King of Ontario were each elected from Prince Albert after being defeated in elections at home.

ESTERHAZY

A Hungarian count, Paul Esterhazy, led Hungarian farmers to this part of southeastern Saskatchewan in 1886. Today Esterhazy is more famous as the home of the world's largest potash mine.

BATTLEFORD AND NORTH BATTLEFORD

Battleford was one of the most important places in Saskatchewan before there was Saskatchewan. It began as a trading post and a riverboat stop, and in 1876, it became a North-West Mounted Police fort and the capital of the whole of the North-West Territories. But the government moved to Regina in 1882. And when the railway bypassed Battleford, the newer community of North Battleford began to replace it.

URANIUM CITY

This town in the far northwestern corner of Saskatchewan was a boom town from the 1950s until the

1980s. Gold and then uranium were discovered in the area, and until 1982, the mines at Uranium City helped to make Canada the world's largest producer and exporter of this nuclear fuel. When the market for uranium declined, Uranium City's mines closed and the town began to shrink.

GRAVELBOURG

The Métis are not Saskatchewan's only francophone people. Father Louis Gravel led settlers from Quebec and New England to Gravelbourg, in the southwestern part of the province, in 1906. Soon the community had a college, a hospital, and a francophone Catholic bishop. Gravelbourg continues to be the centre of francophone life in Saskatchewan.

The Saskatchewan Indian Federated College, in Saskatoon, is the only aboriginal university in Canada.

The Capture of Batoche, 1885.

BATOCHE

Batoche, a small village where a ferry crossed the North Saskatchewan River, was founded in 1872 by a Métis family who had moved west from Manitoba. Other Métis families soon joined them, and their town became the centre of the Saskatchewan Métis community. In 1884–85, Batoche was the headquarters of the resistance against the Canadian government. Gabriel Dumont led the defence throughout a three-day siege in May 1885. When the town fell, the Métis' armed resistance was finished.

CO-OP WORKERS

Farm families banded together in 1924 to found the Saskatchewan Wheat Pool, which would store and market their grain. Today the wheat pool is active in many farm businesses. It publishes a newspaper (called the *Western Producer*) and books, and it promotes agriculture, self-sufficiency, and co-operative development. The co-operative spirit has spread from business to politics.

The Saskatchewan Wheat Pool launched the province's co-operative political tradition.

POTASH MINERS

Potash mines are big industrial operations, though in Saskatchewan they often stand in the midst of wheat fields. Deposits of potash lie deeply buried below the prairie, and the mine shafts must penetrate hundreds of metres down. Several thousand Saskatchewanians work in potash mines. The question of whether the mines should be owned by private companies or by the people of Saskatchewan has often been an issue in provincial elections.

FARMERS

Almost 40 per cent of Saskatchewan's people still live in its rural areas. But today one farm family with a lot of machinery can produce more food than dozens of families once grew. So even though Saskatchewan produces more food than ever before, its rural population has thinned out. With few customers, small-town businesses and services close, and the towns seem to fade away. Saskatchewanians are working hard to overcome these challenges and keep rural Saskatchewan thriving.

POLITICAL WORKERS

They take their politics seriously out on the prairie. With its strong socialist and co-operative traditions, Saskatchewan has always been a source of union organizers, NDP political activists, and left-wing commentators and intellectuals. But there is a counter-trend as well: from John Diefenbaker's day to the rise of the Canadian Alliance, Saskatchewan has also given the country lively conservative thinkers and politicians.

> Every year, Saskatchewan produces about twice as much wheat as all the other provinces combined.

CURLERS

The sport of curling is popular all over Canada, and Canadian curlers have often been world champions and Olympic medallists. But curling is something special in Saskatchewan, and over the years, the province has produced many of Canada's finest rinks (curling teams). Today curling is so popular that some professional rinks spend much of the winter competing for cash prizes at bonspiels (curling tournaments) around the world.

TOMMY DOUGLAS (1904-1986)

Tommy Douglas was an immigrant from Scotland and a Baptist minister. Settling in Weyburn in 1930, he saw the hardships of the Depression and the dust bowl, and they made him a socialist. A lively, funny, passionate speech maker, he was first elected to Parliament in 1935. Nine years later, in 1944, Douglas returned to Saskatchewan and led his CCF party to power. He was the premier of Saskatchewan for seventeen years, until he left to lead the newly founded New Democratic Party in Ottawa. Douglas's legacy to Saskatchewan and Canada was a network of new social services and a model of co-operative action.

GABRIEL DUMONT (1837-1906)

The greatest of the Métis buffalo hunters, Gabriel Dumont could see that the animals were doomed by overhunting, and he tried to help his people settle as farmers around St-Laurent and Batoche. But Canadian surveyors ignored the Métis landholdings as they divided up the land for settlers.

When the Métis decided to fight in 1885, Dumont became their military leader. He was a brilliant guerrilla fighter, but he could not defeat the large, well-equipped Canadian forces that the railway had delivered to the Prairies. After the fall of Batoche, Dumont fled to the United States. He worked for a time as a marksman in Buffalo Bill's Wild West Show, but he returned home to die at Batoche.

GORDIE HOWE (1928-   )

Gordie Howe's family was too poor to afford hockey skates, but when someone gave him a pair, Gordie started skating – and almost never stopped. He was strong as well as skilful, with a powerful will to win. He has been called the greatest athlete who ever played hockey.

KITCHI-MANITOU-WAYA, OR ALMIGHTY VOICE (1874-1897)

Almighty Voice grew up on a Cree reserve near Batoche. He was arrested for a minor crime in 1895, but he escaped from the jail at Duck Lake and killed a police officer. For almost two years, he evaded capture and lived by hunting and gathering. Finally, a hundred police officers and civilians cornered him not far from his home. In a two-day battle, Almighty Voice killed two policemen before cannonfire killed him and two relatives travelling with him.

Almighty Voice near Duck Lake, about 1892.

MISTAHIMASKWA, OR BIG BEAR (1825–1888)

The Plains Cree chief Big Bear was among the last of the leaders of the free-ranging buffalo hunters of the plains. Each year, his people rode from their winter camps along the North Saskatchewan to follow the herds. In 1876, Big Bear, unlike other Plains chiefs, refused to sign a treaty with Canada. He wanted his people to be able to continue their way of life.

But by 1882, with the buffalo almost gone and his people starving, even Big Bear had to sign on. In 1885, with the Métis planning to go to war against the Canadian government, he tried to prevent his people from joining in a hopeless struggle. Angry young warriors rejected his advice. They attacked Canadian troops, and Big Bear was jailed for what his followers had done. He died, a broken man, soon after.

W. O. MITCHELL (1914–1998)

No one did more to capture the Prairies in words than W. O. (William Ormond) Mitchell, and no one has influenced and inspired more Prairie writers. Mitchell spent much of his adult life in Alberta, but Saskatchewan, with its dry, windswept prairie and its tough, caring people, is the setting of his funny and moving novels, plays, and stories, including *Who Has Seen the Wind?* and *Jake and the Kid.*

PITIKWAHANANAPIWIYAN, OR POUNDMAKER (ABOUT 1842–1886)

Poundmaker was another Native leader destroyed by the outcome of the 1885 Métis uprising. Born among the Plains Cree, Poundmaker was adopted by Crowfoot, a chief of the rival Blackfoot nation. In 1879, with the buffalo almost gone, Poundmaker led his people regretfully to a reserve near Battleford. When the uprising broke out, he could not prevent some of his young warriors from joining it. He was charged with treason and died soon after being released from jail.

JEANNE SAUVÉ (1922–1993)

Jeanne Sauvé was a brilliant journalist who became the first female Speaker of the House of Commons and the first woman governor general of Canada. She was also a Saskatchewanian, born in the small francophone community of Prud'homme.

Regina's granite-and-limestone legislature building.

The name Saskatchewan comes from a Cree word first applied to the swift-flowing Saskatchewan River. The name was borrowed from the river for a district of the North-West Territories in 1882. In 1905, it became the name of the new province, although some local people had preferred Assiniboia. Saskatchewan is the only Canadian province or territory whose boundaries are all straight lines (and entirely uninfluenced by geographical features such as mountain ranges or sea coasts).

Today the people of Saskatchewan elect a legislature of fifty-eight men and women, known as members of the Legislative Assembly (MLAs). The party that is supported by a majority of MLAs forms a government, which "advises" the lieutenant-governor, the ceremonial head of the provincial administration. In Ottawa, Saskatchewan is represented by fourteen members of Parliament and six senators.

The Saskatchewan legislative building in Wascana Park at Regina was designed by Edward and William Maxwell of Montreal. It was built of granite and limestone between 1908 and 1912. Saskatchewanians can boast that the dome of their legislature is just over a metre higher than Alberta's.

Two prime ministers, Wilfrid Laurier and Mackenzie King, held seats in Saskatchewan for a time. But the only prime minister actually from Saskatchewan was John G. Diefenbaker, prime minister from 1957 to 1963. As leader of the Progressive Conservatives, "Dief" stood for the little guy and the ordinary voter. He saw himself as an outsider in Ottawa, at least until 1958, when he won the greatest electoral victory ever seen in Canada to that time. Even when he was out of office at the end of his career, he remained a towering figure, beloved particularly in the small towns of Western Canada, where he'd launched his career. He lies buried beside the Diefenbaker Centre in Saskatoon.

Saskatchewan has also given Canada a strong tradition of social action and social democracy. With its emphasis on self-sufficiency, public ownership, and co-operative movements, the province has been a stronghold of the left-wing CCF and New Democratic parties, and it has contributed many leaders and workers to that cause. Saskatchewan was the first Canadian province to elect a socialist government, and it was in Saskatchewan that medicare was first introduced.

LANDS AND TREATIES

As soon as Canada acquired the North-West Territories in 1870, it began to seek treaties with the Native nations of the prairies. Canada wanted these nations to surrender their land in exchange for small reserves and payments, and Canada's representatives pushed the Natives hard to accept those terms. Treaty Four, signed in 1874, covered the southern prairie. Treaty Six, signed at Fort Carleton in 1876, covered the Saskatchewan River country, and later treaties covered northern Saskatchewan.

But not all Native groups accepted the treaties. Mistahimaskwa, or Big Bear, was one of the leaders who made no treaty until all the buffalo were gone. The Métis around Batoche in the 1870s and 1880s also believed they had a right to the land they had settled. The coming of Canadian government surveyors helped touch off the Métis uprising of 1885.

Today the Native and Métis communities are strong in Saskatchewan. The Saskatchewan Indian Federated College, in Saskatoon, is one of Canada's leading Native-run centres of higher education.

Mistahimaskwa, or Big Bear, about 1885.

JOINED CONFEDERATION:
Alberta and Saskatchewan became the eighth and ninth provinces together on September 1, 1905

PROVINCIAL MOTTO:
Multis e gentibus vires (From many peoples, strength)

PROVINCIAL FLOWER:
Prairie lily

AREA:
651,900 square kilometres (almost 7 per cent of Canada)

HIGHEST POINT:
Cypress Hills (1,392 metres above sea level)

POPULATION:
978,933

GROWTH RATE:
Down 1.1 per cent since 1996

CAPITAL:
Regina

MAIN CITIES:
Saskatoon (225,927), Regina (192,800), Prince Albert (41,460), Moose Jaw (33,519)

SASKATCHEWAN GOVERNMENT INFORMATION ON THE INTERNET:
www.gov.sk.ca

THE TOP CROPS

A lot of our food is raised in Saskatchewan. There are about 50,000 farms in the province, and they cover 26 million hectares of land.

But you may be surprised to learn that it's not all fields of wheat. Almost every farm in the province does grow crops of some kind, but many focus on animals such as pigs, cattle, and poultry more than plants. Still, crops and grain elevators continue to symbolize Saskatchewan farms. The top five field crops in the province are:

1. Spring Wheat – 4.3 million hectares. Wheat has been king since settlers first flooded into Saskatchewan a century ago. In 2001, farmers planted 4.3 million hectares with spring wheat, providing bread and flour for hungry people all over the world.

But wheat production has been falling fast. In fact, the production of spring wheat was down 23 per cent in just five years. Why? Many other countries, including China and Russia, also produce wheat, and several of them pay their farmers to sell the crop to the world market at almost any price. Our farmers are looking for other crops that will flourish in the dry prairie landscape.

2. Canola – 1.92 million hectares. Canola is a Canadian invention. Canadian Food scientists wanted to improve the quality of an oilseed crop, and the new variety they created was so much better they gave it a new name in Canada's honour. Today Canola is the second most important crop in Saskatchewan fields by area.

3. Barley – 1.86 million hectares. What would beer drinkers do without Saskatchewan? A lot of barley is malted for beer, but a lot goes for livestock food too. These days, barley is the province's third most important field crop by area.

4. Durum wheat – 1.6 million hectares. Durum is the wheat that makes the flour that goes into your pasta. Our farmers grew 1.6 million hectares of it in 2001.

5. Alfalfa – 1.1 million hectares. What's alfalfa for? It's mostly used to feed dairy cattle, so it's lucky Saskatchewanians grow so much of it. They have three million hungry cattle to feed.

SASKATCHEWAN

MOUNTAINS ABOVE THE PLAIN

Albertans live in the lee of great mountains, warmed by chinook winds. Alberta is feisty, fast-growing, prosperous, and self-reliant. Out of the province come successful sports teams, free-wheeling entrepreneurs, most of Canada's oil and gas, and lively political ideas.

Alberta's two great cities, Edmonton and Calgary, are the fifth and sixth largest in Canada. Calgary thrives on the oil business, ranching, and the financial industry. Edmonton is a centre of transportation, government, and education. But Albertans are country people too, proud of their cowboy boots and pickup trucks. Religion is also important for a lot of Albertans, and many of Canada's leading evangelical Christian preachers got their start in the province.

"The West wants in" was the cry of an Alberta-born political movement of the 1990s. As proud members of one of Canada's largest, wealthiest, and most innovative provinces, Albertans are not willing to be neglected – or pushed about – by anyone. Alberta entered the twenty-first century with almost three million people, a thriving economy, and one of the highest standards of living in Canada.

LANDSCAPES

It may be one of the Prairie provinces, but nobody ever calls Alberta flat. It is backed by the Rocky Mountains, the greatest mountain range in North America, and from Calgary and Lethbridge and other cities, you can see the mighty peaks rising to the west and feel the storm winds and the warm chinooks that roll down off them. Alberta feeds great rivers that flow through foothills, plains, and woodlands, draining to three different oceans. It is farmland, rangeland, woodland, desert, glacier, and more – all in one province.

BADLANDS

Along the Red Deer River near Drumheller, the ground is formed of soft shale and sandstone that crumbles and erodes into plunging cliffs, twisting gullies, and fantastical stone towers and pillars called hoodoos. Albertans call this area the badlands – a bad place to hunt or gather, to raise crops, or to graze farm animals. But it is a fine place to search for dinosaur bones. As cliffs and river-banks erode, new fossils become exposed every year. Dinosaur hunters have been coming to the badlands, particularly Dinosaur Provincial Park, which is a World Heritage Site and one of the world's richest fossil beds, for decades.

DRYLANDS

In southeastern Alberta, the Milk River drains away to the Mississippi basin and the Gulf of Mexico. This is the dry, treeless, short-grass prairie. If you want to farm here, pray for rain or plan to irrigate. Still, this is fine open range for Alberta beef cattle.

PARKLANDS

In central Alberta, the North Saskatchewan River and its tributaries drain away east to Hudson Bay. Much of this is rich farming country

with thick black soils and tall-grass plains interspersed with aspen groves on the rolling hills.

FORESTS

In northern Alberta, the Athabaska River and the Peace River drain away north to the Arctic Ocean. This is the boreal forest, a land of large lakes and great rivers. Once it was rich with beaver. Today its resources draw Albertans north to forestry mills and oil-sands plants.

Lucius O'Brien,
View of the Rockies, *1887.*

MOUNTAINS

The greatest mountains on the continent form Alberta's western boundary. Foothills rise gently to the west and give way to jagged three-thousand-metre peaks, a world of glacier lakes and snowfields, natural parks, and spectacular passes for highways and railways.

1870 Canada acquired the trading territories of the Hudson's Bay Company and established the North-West Territories, including what is now Alberta.

1882 Princess Louise Caroline Alberta, fourth daughter of Queen Victoria and wife of Canada's governor general, the Marquess of Lorne, gave her third name to one of the new administrative districts of the North-West Territories.

1901 With crowds of immigrants – from Eastern Canada, the United States, and Europe – coming to Alberta, the population reached seventy-three thousand. Many Albertans believed it was time the people of the Prairies became full partners in Confederation, able to run their own affairs.

Alberta becomes a province, 1905.

1905 Alberta and Saskatchewan became the eighth and ninth provinces of Canada. Alexander Rutherford, the leader of the Liberal Party, became Alberta's first premier.

1914 Blessed with rains, Alberta's farmers provided rich crops to help support Canada's efforts in the First World War.

1921 Alberta's population had grown to 580,000, but drought threatened the farmers of the drylands. A farmers' political party, the United Farmers of Alberta, won the provincial election.

1929 Premier John Brownlee won the province control of its natural resources, which the federal government had not given up when Alberta joined Confederation.

1935 Depression and drought made life harsh for Alberta's farmers. Many farm families had to abandon the drylands of southern Alberta. The Social Credit Party replaced the United Farmers as Alberta's government. Under William Aberhart, Ernest Manning, and Harry Strom, it remained in power until 1971.

1941 Population growth in Alberta had slowed since the 1920s. The province had 796,000 people.

1947 A gusher erupted at an oil well at Leduc, just east of Edmonton. Alberta began its rise to prosperity as Canada's leading producer of oil and other petrochemical products.

1954 Through the generosity of the oil-rich Harvie family, the Glenbow Museum, one of Canada's great museums and art galleries, opened in Calgary.

1961 There were 1.3 million Albertans. Ranching and farming were still important, but most Albertans now lived in cities.

1971 Peter Lougheed led the Progressive Conservative Party to power, ending thirty-six years of Social Credit rule.

1973 A worldwide oil crisis sent prices soaring. Alberta began to invest some of its oil income in the Alberta Heritage Fund, which grew to be worth billions.

1988 Calgary hosted the athletes of the world at the Winter Olympic Games.

1992 Calgary's mayor, Ralph Klein, became the premier of Alberta, a position he still held at the start of the new millennium.

2002 The heads of government of Canada and seven other leading countries gathered at Kananaskis for the annual meeting of an international body called the Group of Eight.

MINING **OIL** FINANCE

Western Examiner

L. XXI. No. 42   THE WESTERN EXAMINER, CALGARY, SATURDAY, FEB. 22, 1947   Price 10 Cen

At Birth of New Alberta Oil Field

IMPERIAL LEDUC No. 1 WELL—Discovery for a second major Alberta oil field, blowing out its huge billow of burning oil and heavy smoke when the well was completed as a big producer last week.

Striking oil in Leduc.

BLACKFOOT

Masters of the southern plains, the people of the Blackfoot nation called buffalo meat "real meat." They never took much interest in the beaver trade of their neighbours to the north. Three tribes make up the Blackfoot nation – the Piegan, the Blood, and the Blackfoot. With their allies, the Sarcee and the Gros Ventre, they formed the Blackfoot confederacy. The Blackfoot leader Isapo-muxika, or Crowfoot, was a great warrior who grasped the need for peace. Crowfoot led his people from hunting to farming, and from a migratory life to settled reserves. Today many Blackfoot people are ranchers and farmers in south-central Alberta.

PLAINS CREE

Once trappers and hunters of the eastern forest, the Plains Cree moved onto the grasslands when horses and guns became available. They challenged the Blackfoot for control of the buffalo and fought many wars as the animals became scarce. One of their chiefs, Pitikwahananapiwiyan, called Poundmaker, helped make peace with the Blackfoot and was adopted as a son by Crowfoot.

STONEY

"These mountains are our sacred places," said the Stoney chief John Snow. The Stoney peoples lived in the foothills of the Rocky Mountains, hunting, trapping, and pursuing the buffalo herds. Later they were brilliant guides for Canadian travellers and railwaymen seeking passes through the mountains. Unlike their Cree and Blackfoot neighbours, who speak languages of the Algonquian family, the Stoney speak a language of the Siouan family, and they were sometimes called the Rocky Mountain Assiniboine.

MORMONS

Mormons are followers of the Church of Jesus Christ of Latter-day Saints, which was founded in the United States in 1830. In 1887, Charles Ora Card, a son-in-law of the founder of the Mormon Church, led a band of followers north to Alberta. Today Mormons form a majority of the population in the area around Lethbridge, and the Mormon temple at Cardston is the centre of Canadian Mormonism.

HUTTERITES

The Hutterites, members of a religious sect founded in central Europe in the 1500s, settled in Alberta and elsewhere on the Prairies in 1918. Hutterites live in communal villages, called colonies, devoted to farming. When it has grown to about 150 people, a Hutterite colony divides to form a new colony, and so Hutterite communities have gradually spread across the Prairies. Hutterites live plain, simple lives, speaking German, running their own schools, and managing their own affairs. Hutterite colonies have some of the most productive, efficient farms in Alberta.

The children of a Hutterite colony.

SOUTH ASIANS

Since the 1960s, people from every part of the world have immigrated to Canada. Edmonton and Calgary, which had small Chinese and Sikh communities from early in the twentieth century, today have sizeable numbers of South Asians. Alberta is also home to many Ismaili Muslims who, along with other South Asians, were expelled from the African nation of Uganda in the 1970s. Hindus from India, Muslims from Pakistan, and Vietnamese are other South Asians represented in the population today.

SMOKEY CIDER STEAKS

Ranching boomed as soon as the railway arrived to take Alberta beef to market. The great Alberta meal is still a barbecued steak of prime beef, though this pork recipe is a delicious favourite too.

4 pork leg or loin steaks (1 inch/2.5 cm thick)
1/2 cup (125 mL) apple juice
1/2 cup (125 mL) regular barbecue sauce
1/4 cup (50 mL) cider vinegar

1/4 tsp (1 mL) liquid smoke
1/4 tsp (1 mL) crushed dried hot red peppers
4 apples

Place pork in a plastic bag or sealable container. Combine apple juice, barbecue sauce, vinegar, liquid smoke, and crushed peppers and pour over pork. Seal and refrigerate 2 hours or overnight. Turn steaks occasionally.

Preheat the barbecue to a high temperature and place the steaks on the grill. Turn the heat down to a low setting and continue to cook 5 to 6 minutes per side till medium done.

Meanwhile, slice apples into wedges and thread on skewers. Grill alongside steaks during the final 5 minutes. Top steaks with grilled apple wedges and serve with baked potatoes and a green salad.

Bronco busting at the Calgary Stampede.

CALGARY

Calgary, which sits on the Bow River, where the foothills come down to the plain, began life as one of the first North-West Mounted Police posts in 1875. When the railway came through in 1883, Calgary became the headquarters for the ranchers and meatpackers of southern Alberta. They launched the Calgary Exhibition in 1886. It was renamed the Calgary Stampede in 1912 and has been one of the world's greatest rodeos ever since.

Then oil was discovered, and Calgary became the capital of the oil patch as well. The fastest-growing city in Canada in recent decades, Calgary is free-wheeling and fast-paced. The capital of southern Alberta is a (usually friendly) rival to the provincial capital in the north.

EDMONTON

A fur-trading fort on the North Saskatchewan River long before Alberta was born, Edmonton became the province's capital in 1905, the same year the railway reached it. The centre of rich farming country, Edmonton is also home to the University of Alberta.

BANFF

Siding 29 was renamed Banff soon after the Canadian Pacific Railway came through in 1883. Two years later, Canada established a park reserve around the nearby hot springs, making Banff Canada's first national park. In 1888, the CPR built the Banff Springs Hotel, and visitors have been flocking to the town ever since.

CARLSTADT

Canadians thought the short grass prairie could be farmed; they did not believe the warnings of those who said the region called Palliser's Triangle received too little rain. Carlstadt, a new town on the CPR's main line, was going to be "the star of the prairie." But Carlstadt, later

called Alderson, was in the driest part of the dry prairie. When the rainy years of the early 1900s gave way to the dust-bowl decades of the 1920s and 1930s, Carlstadt dried up and blew away. Today there is only a ghost town along the tracks.

FORT MCMURRAY

Once a fur-trading fort on the Athabaska River, Fort McMurray lies in the heart of the oil sands. Here the oil is mixed with thick, tarry sands, instead of sitting in liquid form in deep underground pools. When efforts to extract the oil began in the 1960s, Fort McMurray boomed. Today the town is the headquarters of the northern oil industry, and home to one of the largest Newfoundlander communities outside Newfoundland.

Dust storms like this one spelled the end for some Alberta towns.

HEAD-SMASHED-IN BUFFALO JUMP

Buffalo fed, clothed, and housed the people of the plains and foothills for ten thousand years. Every year, the hunting peoples came to Head-Smashed-In, near Fort Macleod, for a carefully planned drive that sent hundreds of buffalo over the cliffs to their deaths. Today the bone beds at the foot of the cliffs are ten metres high, and an interpretation centre recreates that era.

A buffalo jump, 1867.

ALBERTA AT WORK

Mining the oil sands in Fort McMurray.

ENERGY WORKERS

Alberta is Canada's leading producer of energy products. Energy workers may be oil-well drillers in the field, refinery workers in Edmonton, heavy-machinery operators in the northern oil-sands plants, or office staff in the towers of Calgary. Alberta has most of Canada's petroleum resources and almost three-quarters of its coal.

SCIENTIFIC WORKERS

During the oil-fuelled prosperity of the 1980s, Alberta decided to invest in new technology and diversify its economy. Today scientific research in petrochemicals, medicine, and other fields employs more Albertans than ever.

FARM WORKERS

Ranching is still big business in southwestern Alberta, and the province is Canada's leading producer of beef. Farther north, farmers produce wheat, barley, canola, and mixed crops, and they raise dairy cattle and poultry.

A fishing industry in landlocked Alberta? The whitefish catch from Alberta's northern lakes is worth more than $5 million a year.

ALBERTA AT WORK

MOUNTAIN GUIDES

For more than a century, Alberta's spectacular mountains and resorts have been drawing visitors from all over the world. In the 1880s, the Canadian Pacific Railway brought skilled mountain guides from Switzerland to Banff, and they became the mentors of the first generation of Canadian mountaineers. Today highly trained park wardens and rescue personnel frequently assist hikers and climbers in Alberta's mountains, and members of the Alpine Club of Canada maintain climbers' huts close to many of the most challenging climbs in the Rockies. In 1982, a Calgary mountain guide, Laurie Skreslet, became the first Canadian to climb Mount Everest, the world's highest peak.

PALEONTOLOGISTS

In the Red Deer River valley badlands, a bone-dry landscape of cliffs, gullies, and towering hoodoos (columns of rock), the scientist Joseph Tyrrell came exploring in the 1880s. He found one of the world's great deposits of dinosaur bones, including the remains of a smaller cousin of *Tyrannosaurus rex* that he named *albertosaurus*. Tyrrell's legacy is the Royal Tyrrell Museum of Paleontology, near Drumheller, the largest dinosaur museum in the world.

RAT CATCHERS

There are rats on Canada's Pacific coast, but they cannot cross the mountains. There are rats in Saskatchewan and south of the border too, but they don't get into Alberta either. The Norway rat, that pesky intruder, has never made it into this province (though kangaroo rats and other native species do live here), and Albertans intend to keep it that way. All along the threatened borders, government rat catchers inspect farms, set out pesticides, and generally make sure that rats never find a welcome in friendly Alberta. So far, it has worked. (By the way, pet rats are illegal in Alberta too.)

Ralph Steinhauer,
who became
lieutenant-governor of
Alberta in 1974,
was the first aboriginal
to hold that
position in Canada.

WILLIAM ABERHART (1878-1943)

They called him "Bible Bill," and by 1930, the teacher and minister from Ontario had become the most popular radio preacher in Alberta. When the Great Depression hit in 1929, Bill Aberhart began seeking solutions. He turned to Social Credit, a theory that in hard times the government could borrow all the money needed to help people. The Social Credit League swept to power in 1935, and Aberhart became premier of Alberta. He died in 1943, but Social Credit ruled Alberta until 1971.

ISAPO-MUXIKA, OR CROWFOOT (ABOUT 1830-1890)

Crowfoot got his name after a feat of bravery in battle against the Crow Indians. But his fame came as a peacemaker. He made peace between his Blackfoot and the rival Cree. Then he led his people through the difficult transition from being free-ranging hunters to living on reserves.

K.D. LANG (1961-   )

k.d. lang (she never uses her given names, Kathy Dawn, or capital letters) from Consort, in ranching country, has a brilliant voice, a lively style, and a flair for publicity, and she rose fast to the top in popular music. She annoyed Alberta's ranchers by promoting vegetarianism, and she was one of the first popular celebrities to "come out" as a lesbian.

PETER LOUGHEED (1928-   )

Peter Lougheed, a Calgary lawyer, brought the Progressive Conservative Party back into power in Alberta in 1971, after thirty-six years of Social Credit rule. The price of oil rose dramatically in the 1970s, and Premier Lougheed encouraged the development that brought prosperity to the province. But he also supported new industries, especially scientific and medical projects, during his fourteen years in office. Before he retired in 1985, Lougheed was considered one of Western Canada's most powerful and orespected leaders.

EMILY MURPHY (1868-1933)

Emily Murphy, who wrote popular books under the name of Janey Canuck, was a great crusader for women's rights, and she became Canada's first woman magistrate. In 1929, she and four other Alberta women took what was called the Persons Case all the way to the Privy

Council in Britain. The case successfully challenged the Canadian Supreme Court's ruling that women were not persons under the law, and therefore could not be appointed to the Canadian Senate. But Emily Murphy did not defend the rights of everyone: she fought hard to keep blacks and Asians out of Canada.

SI'K-OKSKITSIS, OR CHARCOAL (ABOUT 1856-1897)

A warrior of the Blood nation, Charcoal was a healer and a mystic. Like many Native Albertans in the late 1800s, he struggled to adapt to a new life of farming on a small reserve. In 1896, he killed a rival. Feeling his own life was over, Charcoal decided he must kill an important person to lead him to the spirit world. One of his victims was an NWMP officer, William Wilde, and a great manhunt followed. Eventually, Charcoal was captured and sentenced to death. He was hanged at Fort Macleod in 1897.

DAVID WALSH (1945-1998)

A hard-luck mining promoter in Calgary, David Walsh thought he had struck it rich when one of his companies, Bre-X Explorations, announced it had found a fabulously rich gold mine in Indonesia. In 1996 and 1997, everyone in the world wanted a piece of Bre-X. Then came disaster: the gold discovery was revealed as a hoax. Bre-X collapsed, and thousands of investors lost the fortunes they thought they had made. Walsh fled to the Bahamas, with everyone who had lost money chasing him. He died there in 1998.

John Ware and his family, about 1896.

JOHN WARE (1845-1905)

He was "the best rough-rider in the North-West." Born a slave, John Ware came north from Texas with the great cattle drives and settled in Alberta in 1882. With his own brand and his own ranch, he raised a family and was popular and respected for his strength, his good humour, and his skill with cattle and horses. John Ware died a rancher's death: his horse stumbled in a gopher hole and fell on him. Ranchers across Alberta mourned his loss.

The Alberta legislature in Edmonton.

The name Alberta comes from Princess Alberta, a daughter of Queen Victoria. It was first given to a district of the former North-West Territories in 1882, and it became the name of the new province when it was established in 1905.

Albertans govern themselves through a legislature of eighty-three elected members. The leader of the party with the greatest number of members becomes premier and appoints a Cabinet of ministers to run the government. The lieutenant-governor signs into law bills passed by the legislature. The Alberta legislature in Edmonton was designed by A. M. Jeffers and built in 1907–13. Jeffers chose a classical style of architecture similar to that then being used for many American state legislatures.

In the Canadian Parliament in Ottawa, Albertans are represented by twenty-eight MPs and six senators. Two Albertans, both Conservatives, have been prime minister – Richard B. Bennett (1930–35) and Joe Clark (1979–80). Albertans have also helped to found two political parties that have been important in national politics: Social Credit in the 1930s and the Reform Party in the 1980s. Reform was co-founded by Preston Manning, whose father, Ernest Manning, was the Social Credit premier of Alberta for many years.

There has always been a strong tradition of independence in the province. In the late 1800s, Alberta Native confederacies negotiated a series of numbered treaties with the federal government, yielding land title to Canada in exchange for reserves and other rights. Today these nations continue to control their own lands and govern their own affairs. A few reserve communities have even grown wealthy from oil and ranching. But others struggle to secure their rights and provide for their people.

This same fierce desire for independence can be seen in the politics of the province. Albertans have always given strong support to governments that appear to be willing to stand up to Ottawa and Eastern Canadian interests. They generally favour politicians who advocate small governments and low taxes. In fact, Alberta is the only province in Canada where shoppers pay no sales tax when they buy things.

Some Albertans think their province and the other Western provinces will become stronger by taking power away from Toronto and Ottawa. Others want to change Canada itself, and they seek ways to give Albertans more influence within the federal government. For both sides, there is a strong sense of alienation and imbalance. "Toronto and Ottawa are a long way away from Alberta," people complain. "Central Canada does not listen, and the West does not have the influence it deserves." Although you can hear charges like these across Western Canada, Alberta often seems to be the province doing the most to make a change.

The province's place in Canada is changing. The population is growing rapidly, and the wealth and influence of Alberta business has expanded hugely, not only in oil and gas but also in many other fields. Many Alberta thinkers and politicians want to be proud Canadians, making their full contribution to Canadian life, and they continue to come up with proposals to address that nagging sense of "Western alienation."

JOINED CONFEDERATION:
Alberta and Saskatchewan became the eighth and ninth provinces together on September 1, 1905

PROVINCIAL MOTTO:
Fortis et liber (Strong and free)

PROVINCIAL FLOWER:
Wild rose

AREA:
661,000 square kilometres

HIGHEST POINT:
Mount Columbia (3,747 metres)

POPULATION:
2,974,807

GROWTH RATE:
10.3 per cent since 1996 (the fastest growth rate in Canada)

CAPITAL:
Edmonton

MAIN COMMUNITIES:
Edmonton (937,847), Calgary (951,395 in 2001 recently replaced Edmonton as Canada's fifth-largest city), Lethbridge (67,324), Red Deer (67,707), Medicine Hat (61,735)

ALBERTA GOVERNMENT INFORMATION ON THE INTERNET:
www.gov.ab.ca

CHINOOK COUNTRY

"In Chinook Country we don't have a climate – we have weather," quipped the Alberta writer Sid Marty. Chinook Country is on the east slope of the Rocky Mountains in southern Alberta, and the chinook is a wind. Yes, winds do have names. There's one called the *föhn* in southern Germany, and the famous sirocco, which blows across the Mediterranean from North Africa to Europe. The chinook was named by a Scottish fur trader in about 1840.

The chinook blows from the southeast in winter or spring – and when it starts to blow, things change fast. It is a warm wind, even though it comes down from the cold and snowy mountains. How is that possible? The wind warms up as it sheds moisture in the tall peaks, and it warms up even more when it is compressed coming down to lower altitudes. That's what the scientists say, anyway. Chinook Country old-timers claim that the racing wind heats up by friction as it rubs across the mountain peaks.

Whatever the explanation for it, the chinook comes fast. Chinook winds have been clocked at more than a hundred kilometres an hour. Chinook Country people say if you drive away from the wind, your front wheels will need snow tires and your rear wheels will be kicking up dust.

If you have been freezing at 30 below on a grim February day, the chinook can feel wonderful. When it blows in, the temperature can rise by twenty to thirty degrees in no time at all. And because it is warm and dry, the chinook melts snow like a hair blower on ice cubes. But it also has a downside. The dry wind draws the moisture of the melting snow up into the air and carries it away. As a result, the ground stays dry and crops die of thirst. That's dry country on the eastern slope of the mountains. The chinook is also a wind that leaves its mark. You can see it in the tilting trees, the wind-carved hoodoo hillsides, and the lined, dusty faces of cowboys who have to ride into it.

BRITISH COLUMBIA

YUKON

CASSIAR MOUNTAINS

WILLISTON LAKE

PRINCE RUPERT

MASSET

SKEENA RIVER

QUEEN CHARLOTTE ISLANDS

KITIMAT

PRINCE GEOR

FRASER RIVER

SKIDEGATE

NINSTINTS

COAST MOUNTAINS

CAPE SCOTT

PORT HARDY

KAMLOO

VANCOUVER ISLAND

STRAIT OF GEORGIA

PACIFIC OCEAN

WHISTLER

NOOTKA

CUMBERLAND

VANCO

NANAIMO

VICTORIA

Although broad plains and grass-land plateaus form part of the landscape, it is those sky-scraping, neck-craning mountains that British Columbians miss most when they leave their province. In much of B.C., people live in steep-sided, forested valleys or on coastal ledges hemmed in by towering peaks.

British Columbia is also a province of coastlines, where deep, glacier-cut fjords run far inland between towering mountains. Stretched out, the province's tangled coastline would reach around the world. The coast is a place of islands and inlets, ferries and fishing boats.

The coast has cities too. Almost three-quarters of British Columbians live around the part of the Georgia Strait that lies between Vancouver, on the mainland, and Victoria and Nanaimo, on Vancouver Island. That represents a lot of people: British Columbia is the third-largest Canadian province in population as well as area.

British Columbia grew and prospered on its natural resources: its mines, its forests, its fish, and also its rivers (which have been harnessed for electrical power). Today's British Columbians worry and debate about these industries. Will the stocks of timber and fish and power be enough for the future? Is clear-cutting destroying the forest? Are the salmon overfished? Is nature being overwhelmed?

The cities of British Columbia look out to the Pacific and the world. Ever since the railway reached the coast in 1885, the province has been Canada's gateway to Asia and the Pacific. Canada's first Japanese, Chinese, and South Asian immigrants all came to British Columbia, and today Asian business is a very important part of the province's economy.

LANDSCAPES

There are more First Nations languages in British Columbia than in all the rest of Canada – because the landscape divided the province into isolated worlds separated by great mountains. Its peoples are more united now, but they still live in a rugged, untameable landscape of fjords and mountains, deserts and rainforests, wild rivers and surf-pounded coasts.

The ferns and mosses of the coastal rainforest.

TEMPERATE RAINFORESTS

Rainforests need not be tropical jungles. British Columbia's coastal forest is one of the most spectacular temperate rainforests in the world. Clouds sweep in from the cold North Pacific, and rain (up to three hundred centimetres a year!) floods down upon the coastal mountains. The rain helps produce a dense underbrush of ferns and mosses close to the ground, and an evergreen forest of cedars and firs rises tall and thick above.

MOUNTAIN BARRIERS

The Rockies are the longest mountain range in North America, with the tallest mountains, but they are only one of British Columbia's several ranges. The province's mountains are "young" by a geologist's vast time scale. Thrust up "only" about sixty million years ago, the western mountains remain steep and jagged, for they have not been eroded and rounded as older mountains have. Many of them soar three thousand metres and more. The tallest of them is Mount Robson, at 3,954 metres.

Most of the province's great rivers – the Fraser, the Columbia, the Kootenay, and the Liard – rise up in the Rocky Mountain Trench, the longest valley in North America. Their twisting routes carry these rivers through the Purcell, Selkirk, Monashee, Cariboo, and Coast ranges before they find the Pacific. The Peace River lies in the corner of British Columbia that is northeast of the mountains. It flows east to Alberta and north towards the Arctic.

ISLAND WORLDS

On the sheltered coastal islands, particularly those of the Gulf of Georgia, between Vancouver Island and the mainland, the salt-loving arbutus tree, or madronna, grows. The arbutus is the only Canadian evergreen with leaves instead of needles, and it never grows far from salt water. The people of British Columbia's hundreds of coastal islands have the same close link with the sea. Sheltered from urbanization by isolation and protective legislation, the islands are havens not just for campers and cottagers, but for artists, small-scale farmers, and crafts-people as well.

DRYLANDS

East of the Coast Range are British Columbia's drylands. Only about twenty-five centimetres of rain falls in the Okanagan Valley each year. It has the same hot summers and cool winters as the Prairie provinces. With irrigation, the Okanagan has become an important fruit-growing and wine-making district, however, while lakeshore beaches and mountainside ski hills make this region a favourite holiday destination. But away from the lakes and beyond the irrigation pipes, this part of British Columbia is a land of rattlesnakes and sagebrush, not mosses and rain.

Farther north, much of the dryland is cattle country. British Columbia has a strong cowboy tradition, and vast ranches dot the Cariboo plateau district.

1849   The Hudson's Bay Company had opened a trading post, Fort Victoria, on Vancouver Island in 1843, and it got permission to bring colonists to the area. The HBC head, James Douglas, became governor of the British colony of Vancouver Island.

1858   News of gold in the Fraser River brought thousands of prospectors, who became the first non-Native settlers on the mainland. To keep order, Britain created the colony of British Columbia. Its governor was James Douglas, who also remained in charge of the other colony, Vancouver Island.

1866   The twin colonies of Vancouver Island and British Columbia were joined together – as British Columbia.

1871   British Columbia officials contemplated making their colony a province of the new Confederation. When Canada promised a transcontinental railway within ten years, British Columbia became the sixth province. Canada's motto, "From Sea to Sea," became a reality.

1881   Ten years after British Columbia joined Confederation, railway construction was just getting started. In the B.C. mountains, surveyors wondered if a route would ever be found. There were about twenty-five thousand settlers in British Columbia, and they were still outnumbered by the Native peoples.

1885   The Canadian Pacific Railway drove "the last spike" at Craigellachie in Eagle Pass. The first train soon reached the Pacific at Port Moody, on Burrard Inlet.

1886   Two months after Vancouver was incorporated, a brush fire roared in and destroyed almost the entire city. The citizens quickly rebuilt. When the railway tracks reached Vancouver, it became the CPR's western terminal and the seaport city of Western Canada.

1914   Premier Richard McBride won popularity by promising to "keep British Columbia white," and immigrants were treated with suspicion. When more than three hundred Sikhs arrived at Vancouver from India aboard the ship *Komagatu Maru*, British Columbians

Driving "the last spike," 1885.

prevented them from disembarking. After two months in Vancouver harbour, they sailed unwillingly for home.

1938   The Lion's Gate Bridge, a slim, spectacular suspension bridge at the entrance to Vancouver harbour, opened for traffic.

1942   During the Second World War, Canada agreed to expel all residents of Japanese origin from the West Coast. Their property and belongings were plundered to pay the cost of the deportation. It would be fifty years before any apology or compensation was made.

1952   William Andrew Cecil Bennett ("Wacky" to his enemies), leader of the Social Credit Party, started a twenty-year run as premier. Bennett spent lavishly on highways, power dams, and ferries, opening much of the province to travel and development.

1972   Dave Barrett, the colourful leader of the New Democratic Party, defeated W. A. C. Bennett and became premier of B.C.'s first left-wing government.

1983   The fiscal restraint program of the next Social Credit premier, Bill Bennett (W. A. C.'s son), reduced government, cut spending on social services, and weakened labour unions. A protest movement, called Solidarity, brought British Columbia closer to a general strike (when all working people go out in protest against the government) than any province in Canada had come since the Winnipeg General Strike of 1919.

1986   A world's fair, Expo 86, brought millions of people to Vancouver. After the fair, new buildings, parks, and museums brightened up the rundown False Creek district of the city, where the fair had been held.

> British Columbia needs many ferries to connect its coastal settlements together. British Columbians like to say that the province has more ships than the Canadian navy.

1998   After years of courtroom battles, the Gitksan and Wet'suwet'en peoples of northwest British Columbia won a Supreme Court of Canada ruling recognizing their right to their land. Soon after, British Columbia reached a broad treaty with the nearby Nisga'a people.

PEOPLES

HAIDA

The Haida are the people of Haida Gwaii, also known as the Queen Charlotte Islands. They were a sea-going people, fishing and hunting in the open ocean and sending trade or war parties along the mainland coasts. Terrible epidemics of smallpox and other diseases reduced their numbers in the 1860s, and today most Haida live in two communities, Skidegate and Masset. But the Haida continue to manage and protect their village sites, including the World Heritage Site at Ninstints. They offer visitors tours of their islands in magnificent Haida canoes. "We have ten thousand years' experience," they proudly declare.

CHINESE

A few Chinese workers came to the northwest coast when sea-otter pelts were being shipped to Canton in the 1770s. But Chinese immigration to British Columbia really began with the gold rush in 1858. Young labourers were brought in to help build the railway through the mountains, and many died performing the dangerous work. Soon, however, most Western towns had a few Chinese businesses, and larger centres usually had a "Chinatown." Yet Canadians feared the Chinese, whose appearance and culture were very different from their own. They were called unfit to be citizens and treated harshly.

At the end of the twentieth century, a new wave of Chinese immigrants arrived. These were wealthy, highly educated Chinese who came to Vancouver (and other parts of Canada) seeking security and opportunity. Today Chinese Canadians are some of the most prosperous and influential people in British Columbia.

A Chinese work gang on the CPR.

Chinese-style artifacts have been found along the British Columbia coast. Did Asian sailors visit Western Canada long before European explorers did?

DOUKHOBORS

Members of the religious sect called Doukhobors (which means "spirit-wrestlers") were persecuted in Russia, and many fled to Canada around 1900. They travelled first to Saskatchewan and later moved on to British Columbia, where they settled around Grand Forks and in the Kootenay region. Doukhobors were fiercely committed to their language and leaders, their communally owned farms, and their traditional way of life. Today conventional Doukhobor society has fewer committed adherents, but the Russian language and other cultural traditions survive.

SIKHS

Sikhs, members of a minority religious group from India's Punjab region, began immigrating to British Columbia in small numbers in 1902. Despite restrictions intended to keep them out of Canada, Sikhs slowly developed their own community. Today they are divided between those who have assimilated into Western society and those who strictly preserve Sikh dress, Sikh culture, and the Sikh religion.

JAPANESE

The turning point for the Japanese community in British Columbia came in 1942. That year, all twenty thousand members were rounded up and shipped away from their West Coast homes, and their property and belongings were confiscated and sold. Until then, most Japanese had been market gardeners or fishers on the British Columbia coast, and the Japanese-Canadian community was a tightly knit, though isolated, one. After the Second World War, however, as some of the exiles returned to British Columbia, the younger Japanese Canadians became businesspeople, professionals, and scholars. Today Japanese Canadians are among British Columbia's most prosperous citizens, and they're highly integrated into Canadian society.

Japanese internees at a camp in Slocan.

NANAIMO BARS

There's a story that when English miners came to Nanaimo to dig coal, relatives back home would ship them sweet bars like these, knowing they would keep well on the long voyage. Nanaimo bars have a bottom crust, a sweet middle, and a chocolate top.

1/2 cup (125 mL) butter
1/4 cup (50 mL) sugar
5 tbsp (75 mL) cocoa
1 egg
1 tsp (5 mL) vanilla
1 2/3 cups (400 mL) fine graham wafer crumbs
1 cup (250 mL) desiccated coconut
1/2 cup (125 mL) chopped walnuts
1/4 cup (50 mL) butter
2 cups (500 mL) sifted icing sugar

1 egg
4 squares semi-sweet chocolate
1 tbsp (15 mL) butter

In a saucepan, combine 1/2 cup (125 mL) butter, sugar, cocoa, 1 egg, and vanilla. Cook over medium heat, stirring constantly, until smooth and slightly thickened. Stir in graham wafer crumbs, coconut, and walnuts and press into a greased 9-inch (23 cm) square cake pan.

For the middle layer, cream 1/4 cup (50 mL) butter. Gradually beat in icing sugar and 1 egg. Spread over the bottom layer and chill for about 15 minutes.

For the top layer, melt together the chocolate squares and 1 tbsp (15 mL) butter. Spread over top of other layers, chill, cut into squares, and serve.

*Victoria's picturesque
Empress Hotel.*

VICTORIA

Victoria is British Columbia's oldest city and the province's capital.
Founded as a Hudson's Bay Company trading post in 1843, it has
always been a seaport. For a long time, it was the most "English" corner of Canada, supposedly a place for tea and tweed suits and lawn
bowling. The city has a mild, English climate too, which attracts retired
people from all over the country.

VANCOUVER

From a few sawmills and taverns in the 1880s, Vancouver grew rapidly
into Canada's third-largest city and the centre of West Coast culture.
Vancouver is unforgettable: the line of north shore mountains, the vast
outer harbour, the inner harbour sealed by the green expanse of Stanley
Park, and what the poet Earle Birney called "the long tamed whale of
Point Grey" stretching into the Gulf of Georgia.

PORT HARDY

Towns on the British Columbia coast lie squeezed between the dark
forest and the cold ocean waters, and they are frequently shrouded in
cloud and rain. Port Hardy, facing the mainland from the north coast

of Vancouver Island, grew up around a cannery, a copper mine, and the forestry industry. Visitors come to catch the ferry to Prince Rupert, and they stay for the fishing and the views. The rugged north coast has attracted many remarkable people. Nearby Sointula ("place of harmony" in Finnish) was founded as a utopian community around 1900, and idealistic Danish settlers tried to found another community at Cape Scott, the rugged, storm-battered point at the northern tip of Vancouver Island.

PRINCE GEORGE

Prince George stands at the geographical centre of British Columbia, at the "big bend," where the Fraser River turns around and begins to flow south towards the sea. The explorer Simon Fraser founded a fur-trade post here in 1807, but lumber and the railway have become the city's main industries. Today Prince George is the largest city in northern British Columbia, with government offices, services, and the newly founded University of Northern British Columbia.

TRAIL

"Never go to Trail, or you'll stink from head to tail," kids in the rest of the Kootenays used to chant. Trail had one of the largest lead-and-zinc smelters in the world, and a lot of dirt came out of the smokestacks. Trail's world-champion amateur hockey team proudly called itself the Smoke-Eaters. Today Trail is much cleaner, but the smelter is still the centre of the community.

Beautiful Whistler.

WHISTLER

Whistler began as a ski hill in the 1960s and blossomed into a city. The ski runs now extend across two mountains, Whistler and Blackcomb. They draw skiers from all over the world and win awards for the best skiing in North America. Down in the valley, Whistler is a year-round resort. Hiking, boating, golf, hotels, and a convention centre keep the town busy.

SEAPLANE PILOTS

In Vancouver's busy harbour, crowded with cruise liners, grain tankers, and ferries, small aircraft are constantly splashing down or swooping up. Despite all the highways, railways, and airports of the province, much of its rugged terrain is still accessible only by small plane. The float plane and the helicopter remain standard transport, carrying loggers, fishers, miners, and many other British Columbians to the woodland clearings or isolated coves where they earn their living.

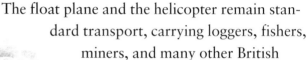

TREE PLANTERS

The forest industry has been British Columbia's biggest industry – but also its most controversial. Are the forests being stripped and ruined forever to provide cheap timber to the United States and Japan? Or can science make the forests a permanently renewable crop? Tree planters live with these questions every day. They walk the newly cut hills, planting the small shoots that may one day be a new forest – or a new crop for the pulp mill.

SOFTWARE DESIGNERS

In Vancouver's hot technology centres, some of the leading-edge software for business, entertainment, and the film world is under production. If you play NHL hockey or World Cup soccer on your home computer, it's Vancouver-created software that lets you pick your team, devise a strategy, and try to make the big plays.

SALMON FISHERS

Salmon was the great traditional food source of the coastal and river peoples of British Columbia. When settlers brought canning processes to the coast in the 1860s, B.C. salmon could be shipped to the world, and it soon became one of the province's most important resources. Today salmon fishers are a multicultural mix of Native peoples and members of many immigrant communities. Since salmon must return from the ocean to the particular river where they hatched, overfishing a river, damming it, or polluting it can destroy an entire "run" of salmon permanently.

Salmon fishing on the Fraser River is a multicultural activity.

MARKET GARDENERS

The flat delta of the Fraser River, built up from soils carried down by the raging river, is British Columbia's best, richest farm land. Most of it is devoted to market gardening, producing fresh vegetables and fruits for Vancouver consumers. Gardening used to be "poor people's work," left to the Sto:lo peoples and to Sikhs, Chinese, and Japanese immigrants. Today every inch of the Fraser valley is precious, and those who own the land they work have become wealthy.

EMILY CARR (1871–1945)

Victoria-born Emily Carr studied art in San Francisco, France, and Britain, but her painting became something special only after she came home to the British Columbia forests, seascapes, and Native communities.

Until 1920, Carr was almost unknown, and she supported herself running an apartment house in Victoria. Then Canadians began to discover both her paintings and her books, and she was recognized as one of the country's great artists.

AMOR DE COSMOS (1825–1897)

He was born plain Bill Smith in Nova Scotia, but after he went west as a gold miner, he became Amor De Cosmos – which in Latin means "lover of the universe." Soon after he arrived in Victoria in 1858, he was considered the most colourful eccentric in the colony. He started a newspaper, got into politics, and proclaimed his views with passion and panache. He was for democracy in British Columbia government, and he was for Confederation with Canada. When both were achieved in 1871, Amor De Cosmos became premier.

JACK DEIGHTON (1830–1875)

He was just a sailor who opened a tavern on the wooded shore of Burrard Inlet, but Jack Deighton provided good food and good conversation. Because he talked so much, he became known as "Gassy Jack," and the community became Gastown. Gassy Jack died years before the railway came and Vancouver was founded, but today there is a statue of him in the downtown neighbourhood that is still called Gastown.

ARTHUR ERICKSON (1924–   )

Arthur Erickson, British Columbia's best-known architect, has built impressive public buildings all over the world, including the Canadian embassy in Washington, D.C. Yet his most characteristic buildings are on Vancouver's north shore: private homes, all cedar and glass, that hang from cliffside lots as if they have grown out of the rock and the clouds.

ALBERT "GINGER" GOODWIN (1887–1918)

Ginger Goodwin came from England to mine coal on Vancouver Island,

and soon he began organizing trade unions all over the province. He was sick with tuberculosis when Canada introduced conscription in 1917, but he was still one of the first "called up" for mandatory military service. Goodwin and his friends were sure it was a trick to get rid of him and other socialist radicals. They fled to the woods near Cumberland, where they were fed and sheltered by friends. When Goodwin was shot dead by the police officers who were hunting for him, all the trade unions in B.C. held a one-day protest strike.

PAULINE JOHNSON, OR TEKAHIONWAKE (1861–1913)

Pauline Johnson, the daughter of a Mohawk chief from the Grand River reserve in Ontario, became a famous ambassador for Canada by performing poems about her Native heritage all over the world. She lived in Vancouver near the end of her life. At her request, her ashes were scattered on the seashore at Stanley Park when she died.

Visitors have been admiring and collecting the art of the northwest coast Native nations since the days of the earliest explorers and traders.

GEORGE MANUEL (1921–1989)

Born on the Neskonlith reserve, George Manuel decided as a young man that Natives had to organize themselves to seek their rights. He helped found the National Indian Brotherhood in the 1960s, which became the Assembly of First Nations in 1980. Manuel went on to link Native Canadians into a world organization of indigenous peoples.

BILL MINER (1847–1913)

He had the big, drooping moustache of an old-time bandit. The modest, polite style he used in his robberies won him the nickname the Gentleman Bandit, and he claimed he had invented the phrase "Hands up." After robbing several CPR trains in the British Columbia mountains, Bill Miner was arrested and jailed in 1906. But he soon escaped and fled across the border into the United States.

BILL REID (1920–1998)

Born of a Haida mother and a Scots father, Bill Reid grew up barely aware of his Native heritage. But his interest in Haida culture grew along with his interest in art, and gradually he established himself as both an expert on Haida art styles and one of Canada's great sculptors. His monumental sculptures have been erected around the world.

The train-robber Bill Miner (wrapped in blanket), after his capture at Kamloops in 1906.

LAW AND ORDER

I n British Columbia, important and influential governments of the Native nations have continued to exist in the shadow of the Canadian and provincial governments. Through court victories and treaties, these Native governments have been acquiring more authority over their own affairs in recent years.

British Columbia's colonial history began with a Hudson's Bay Company government in 1849, and with the foundation of the colonies of Vancouver Island and British Columbia. British Columbia negotiated its own terms when it joined Confederation in 1871, and it gained more powers over land and resources than Alberta or Saskatchewan did when the Canadian government made them provinces in 1905.

British Columbians govern themselves through a legislature of seventy-five seats. The party with the greatest number of members provides a premier and a Cabinet. The lieutenant-governor signs into law bills passed by the legislature. In the Canadian Parliament in Ottawa, British Columbia is represented by thirty-three members and six senators.

The legislature building at Victoria overlooks the scenic harbour.

The British Columbia legislature in Victoria was built of local granite in 1893–97. With its imperial dome and grand entrance arch, it has dominated the view across Victoria's inner harbour ever since. The building made its architect, twenty-five-year-old Francis Rattenbury, famous. He went on to design many of the province's courthouses, banks, and hotels, including the Parliament's close neighbours, Victoria's famous Empress Hotel and the Crystal Gardens pavilion. Rattenbury eventually moved to England, where he was murdered in 1935.

British Columbia has often had the liveliest, most confrontational politics in Canada. It is a province deeply divided between conservative supporters of free enterprise, low taxes, and small government and left-wing supporters of public enterprises and government leadership in both social and economic programs. There has not been much room in between. The Social Credit Party, the main conservative party, has dominated provincial politics for half a century, but British

Columbians often elect New Democratic Party politicians to the federal legislature.

In recent years, British Columbia has provided two very short-lived prime ministers of Canada. John Turner, who grew up in British Columbia but made his career in Montreal and Toronto, became prime minister in 1984, but his Liberal Party was defeated in a general election a few months later. Vancouverite Kim Campbell became leader of the Progressive Conservative Party and Canada's first woman prime minister in 1993. She too saw her party defeated in a general election a few months later, and she even lost her own seat in Vancouver.

LAND CLAIMS

In the 1870s, as Canada expanded into the prairie West, the government made treaties with the Native nations. These treaties guaranteed Canada's title to the land, and in exchange, the Native peoples received some reserve land and various promises and payments. The treaties were often one-sided, unfair, and barely understood by the people signing them. But they did establish Canada's title, and they did confirm that Canada had obligations towards the original inhabitants.

When British Columbia joined Canada in 1871, no treaties like these were signed in most of the province. Many of the Native nations have continued to insist that since they never surrendered the land in a treaty, their claim is as good as British Columbia's.

Canada and British Columbia ignored this problem for more than a century – though Native leaders never forgot it. During the 1990s, Canadian courts began to accept the arguments of the Nisga'a, the Gitksan, and other Native communities. In 1998–99, the Nisga'a, British Columbia, and Canada agreed upon one of the first large land-claims treaties ever made in the province.

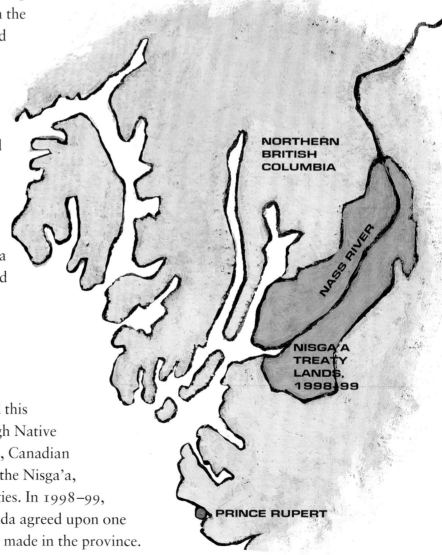

NORTHERN BRITISH COLUMBIA

NASS RIVER

NISGA'A TREATY LANDS, 1998-99

PRINCE RUPERT

JOINED CONFEDERATION:
July 20, 1871 (the sixth province)

PROVINCIAL MOTTO:
Splendor sine occasu (Unlimited splendour)

PROVINCIAL FLOWER:
Pacific dogwood

AREA:
948,596 square kilometres (almost 10 per cent of Canada)

HIGHEST POINT:
Mount Fairweather (4,663 metres above sea level)

POPULATION:
3,907,738

GROWTH RATE:
4.9 per cent since 1996

CAPITAL:
Victoria

MAIN CITIES:
Vancouver (1,986,965 in 2001), Victoria (311,902), Prince George (85,035), Kamloops (86,491), Kelowna (147,739), Nanaimo (85,664), Penticton (41,574)

BRITISH COLUMBIA GOVERNMENT INFORMATION ON THE INTERNET:
www.gov.bc.ca

THE THINGS THAT PEOPLE SEE IN LAKE OKANAGAN

Perhaps more than any other people, the First Nations have understood that there are spirits in the hills, in the trees, in the animals that surround us. They have also understood the presence, all over Canada, of something deep and dark in our lakes – and the need for that presence to be respected. If accidents or deaths occurred in those waters, their awe only increased.

The most famous "presence" in a Canadian lake is N'ha-a-itk. British Columbians know it better as Ogopogo – the creature in Lake Okanagan. For the Salish Natives who lived around Lake Okanagan, N'ha-a-itk was for centuries a force to be both feared and respected. But European newcomers largely discounted their tales – until Ogopogo was spotted by Susan Alliston, an early settler, in 1872. With that sighting, the story was launched among non-Native Canadians, and now several people a year claim to see something in the lake. And every year, Ogopogo stories are a great boon to the Okanagan tourist trade. Here are a few quick facts about Canada's version of the Loch Ness Monster:

- Ogopogo got its name from a silly English song early in the twentieth century. It had no local connections at all until then.
- Ogopogo appeared on a Canadian postage stamp in 1990.
- Ogopogo's home was originally near Kelowna. Now it is "seen" all along Lake Okanagan.
- Ogopogo is officially under the protection of the British Columbia government and may not be hunted.
- Ogopogo tends to be seen most clearly by photographers when the lens cap is still on their cameras.
- Ogopogo's cousins in other Canadian lakes include Cadborosaurus ("seen" at Cadboro Bay, near Victoria) and a creature in Lake Memphremagog in Quebec.

MORE THAN
THE GOLD MINERS

T he Yukon River, one of North America's largest, is a broad, slow-moving stream that drains much of the Yukon Territory before crossing into Alaska on its way to the Bering Sea. Athapaskan-speaking peoples have long made the valley of the Yukon and the territory between the Mackenzie Mountains on the east and the St. Elias range on the southwest their home.

As a territory of Canada, Yukon burst onto the map in 1898, with the great Klondike gold rush. For some, Yukon is still the last frontier, a place to seek paydirt and get out. Today about 80 per cent of Yukoners are non-aboriginals. Many young Canadians go north to work in mining, tourism, and government, and some stay only briefly before returning south.

But for both the Native communities and a growing number of Yukon residents, life in the territory is not a flash in the pan. Yukon today is the busy modern city of Whitehorse, the tourist attractions of Dawson, the mines of Faro, and the traditional ways of "the communities." Passenger jets share airport space with bush planes, while recreation vehicles and powerful trailer transports eat each other's dust along the Alaska Highway. And far from the crowds, there are still many quiet valleys for the moose and the wolves, and maybe also a few nuggets of gold waiting to be discovered.

LANDSCAPES

"I t's a dry cold," Yukoners will tell a visitor. Yukon is dry because the St. Elias Mountains block the heavy, wet clouds rolling in from the Pacific. In fact, many places in southern Canada get much more snow than Yukon does. But those mountains also block the moderating effect of ocean currents, and so Yukon has experienced some of the coldest winter temperatures ever recorded in Canada.

AN ARCTIC PLATEAU

Yukon is part of the same rugged Cordilleran Region that forms most of British Columbia, but only parts of the territory are truly mountainous. The Yukon River has few rapids, and paddlewheelers used to travel twenty-eight hundred kilometres up the river from the Pacific coast in Alaska to Whitehorse. Much of central Yukon, through which the river flows, is a high plateau, thinly treed and very cold in winter.

THE COASTAL PLAIN

Northwestern Yukon is one of the few parts of North America that was not covered by glaciers during the ice ages. There was never enough snow for that. This is a cold, dry, treeless tundra, home to polar bears and to the Porcupine caribou herd (it is so large that it has its own name), which migrates between Alaska and the Yukon Territory. In recent years, oil exploration has moved on to the Arctic coast.

A caribou migration.

THE COAST MOUNTAINS

Yukon's great mountains lie in its southwest corner, close to the Pacific

coast and the panhandle of Alaska. Mount Logan is the highest peak in Canada. These mountains formed a daunting barrier to the gold-rush miners who tried to climb the short but very steep Chilkoot Pass to reach the Klondike from Skagway, Alaska.

YUKON'S NATIONAL PARKS

Kluane National Park is full of breathtaking scenery and spectacular wildlife. It comprises parts of the St. Elias mountain range, including Mount Logan, and therefore attracts climbers from around the world. By contrast, hardly anyone visits Vuntut and Ivvavik national parks, near Old Crow in the Far North. Neither park has tourist facilities or even roads – these are wildlife refuges. The two parks provide habitat for the Porcupine caribou herd, and Vuntut is also a wetland of global significance. Millions of migratory birds visit its lakes and marshlands during Yukon's short summer months.

Kluane National Park is a sea of wildflowers in the North's short summer.

1896 On August 17, George Carmack, guided by his Native brothers-in-law, found gold on a stream they soon called Bonanza Creek, a tributary of the Klondike River. It took a year before word of the gold strike reached Victoria, Seattle, San Francisco, and the world. Then one hundred thousand goldseekers rushed towards the Klondike.

Climbing the Chilkoot Pass.

1898 In June, the Yukon Territory was created out of Canada's North-West Territories to assert Canadian sovereignty in the goldfields, as most of the miners coming were Americans entering through Alaska. A military unit, the Yukon Field Force, was established to support the civilian government, and the North-West Mounted Police soon posted 250 Mounties to the North.

1899 Yukoners held their first election and chose two members for the newly established Yukon Territorial Council.

1900 The White Pass and Yukon Railway, from Skagway, Alaska, to Whitehorse, was completed just as the Klondike gold rush began to give out.

1903 The North-West Mounted Police established its northernmost post at Herschel Island, a summertime gathering place for whaling ships on the Arctic coast.

1913 A silver mine opened at Keno Hill. The gold rush was fading, but commercial mining would eventually be the basis of the Yukon economy.

1942 The Alaska Highway, a wartime "megaproject" that was designed to make it easier to supply Allied military forces in Alaska, was started. The 2,451-kilometre road from Dawson Creek, B.C., to Fairbanks, Alaska, was completed in a year by eleven thousand soldiers (mostly American) and sixteen thousand civilians.

1946   Canada took over control of the Alaska Highway from the armed forces and opened it to civilian traffic the following year.

1947   Snag, Yukon, experienced the lowest temperature ever officially recorded in Canada: −63°C.

1953   Whitehorse replaced Dawson City as Yukon's capital, and the territory's elected council began to expand.

1954   Commercial riverboat service between Whitehorse and Dawson City ended as road traffic took over.

1958   Pierre Berton's book *Klondike* renewed interest in Yukon history. In 1962, the Palace Grand Dance Hall was restored, and tourists began to return to Dawson City.

1969   The town of Faro, named for a Las Vegas card game, opened to serve Canada's largest lead-zinc mine and quickly became Yukon's largest town after Whitehorse. Faro almost died when the mine closed in 1982, and despite a brief revival, it had shrunk to almost nothing by the mid-1990s.

1979   For the first time, a premier and a Cabinet answerable to the elected members of Yukon's territorial legislature, rather than a commissioner appointed by Ottawa, took charge of Yukon's internal affairs.

1984   After nine years of negotiation, Yukon First Nations and the Canadian government reached an agreement in principle on Yukon land claims.

1993   The Council of Yukon Indians signed an umbrella agreement, setting the stage for comprehensive land treaties for twenty First Nations groups in Yukon.

T he north slope of the Yukon Territory remained ice-free, even at the height of the ice ages, and archeologists tell us that the Yukon River valley must have been a prime route by which the Americas were peopled. Some of the very first North Americans were Yukoners. Today's Yukon First Nations are mostly descended from bands of Dene-speaking peoples who adapted to the mountains and plateaus of Yukon.

Gwich'in mothers often outfitted their children in caribou-skin garments.

GWICH'IN

The Gwich'in (also called the Kutchin or Loucheux) of northern Yukon are hunters who followed the Porcupine caribou herds of the northern Barren Grounds. Gwich'in women were celebrated for the fine caribou-skin garments they made. When European fur traders first reached Yukon, the Gwich'in became traders themselves, and they carried European goods north to the Inuit and west into Alaska. To this day, the Gwich'in language remains strong in the communities of northern Yukon.

HAN

Traditionally, the Han lived around the site of Dawson City and harvested salmon from the Yukon River every summer (the name Klondike comes from a Han word meaning "salmon traps"). They were almost overwhelmed by the one hundred thousand gold-rush miners of 1898.

TUTCHONE

The Tutchone fished and hunted in the woodlands and mountains of southern Yukon. They traded copper and furs with the peoples of the Pacific coast, and they had many contacts with the Tlingit and other coastal peoples. In 1995, Judy Gingell, a Tutchone, was appointed commissioner of the Yukon Territory.

INUIT

The Arctic coast of Yukon was a highway for Inuit peoples who wanted to move back and forth between Alaska and the coasts and islands of the central Arctic. The Inuit of Yukon have always had close relations with Alaskan peoples. They call themselves Inuvialuit and have remained slightly separate in language, culture, and politics from the Inuit peoples farther east.

GOLDEN BROILED ARCTIC CHAR

Arctic char is a fish of the salmon species that lives in salt water but returns to northern lakes and rivers to spawn. It is a Yukon delicacy that can now be found on the menus of some of the finest restaurants elsewhere in the country.

2 lb (1 kg) Arctic char fillets
1 tbsp (15 mL) chopped onion

2 tbsp (25 mL) lemon juice
1 tsp (5 mL) salt
pinch of pepper
1/4 tsp (1 mL) tarragon
1/4 cup (50 mL) butter

Place char fillets on a greased broiler pan. Mix together all other ingredients and use half the sauce to baste the fish. Broil fillets 2 to 4 inches (5 to 10 cm) from heat source (6 to 8 inches/15 to 20 cm for frozen). When browned, turn over and baste with remaining sauce. Broil 10 minutes for each inch of thickness for fresh char, or 20 minutes per inch for frozen. Garnish with parsley and serve.

WHITEHORSE

Whitehorse is the North's most populous city.

Whitehorse was born as the head of navigation for the steamboats that came up the Yukon River, all the way from the ocean. In 1900 it got a railway link to the coast. In 1935 an airport was opened, and in 1942 the Alaska Highway came by. As the centre of transportation for Yukon, Whitehorse soon became its largest city. In 1953, the capital moved there from the slowly shrinking town of Dawson City, farther north. Sheltered on a hillside plateau above the river, Whitehorse has Yukon's mildest climate.

FARO

Faro is a town named for a card game, and life there has always been a high-stakes gamble. A mining company built the town when it opened a lead-zinc mine in the 1960s, and through the 1970s, Faro boomed. But when the mine closed down in 1982, so did the town. Although they both revived in the late 1980s, the mine was in trouble again by 1994, and it was time for Faro to shrink once more. While it lasted, however, Faro was both a valuable source of jobs and money and a lively little town that even boasted its own folk festival for a while.

OLD CROW

Old Crow is one of the Kutchin communities of northern Yukon, where Kutchin hunting families began to settle permanently early in the twentieth century. It is named for Walking Crow, a chief in the 1870s. The Kutchin still hunt and fish in their traditional territories around the town, and Old Crow is one of the Yukon communities where traditional culture remains strong and vibrant.

Artifacts found in the hills above Old Crow suggest that people lived there twenty thousand or more years ago.

BLUEFISH CAVES

In the hills above the Bluefish River valley, the Canadian archeologist Jacques Cinq-Mars found evidence of mammoth, horses, and bison, and also of the people who hunted them, perhaps eighteen thousand years ago, when most of North America south of here was covered by glaciers. These are among the earliest sites of human habitation ever discovered on the American continents, and archeologists continue to debate their interpretation.

HERSCHEL ISLAND

The northernmost place in Yukon is also one of its older settlements. Named by the explorer John Franklin in 1826, it became an American whaling base, an Anglican mission, and a North-West Mounted Police station. Today Herschel Island is unpopulated, but oil exploration goes on all around it.

DAWSON CITY

Dawson City, five hundred kilometres north of Whitehorse, stands on flats where the Klondike River joins the Yukon River. Han fishers once dried their salmon catch here, but that changed forever when gold was discovered up the Klondike in 1896. Dawson had fifteen thousand people for a few years. Since then, it has been declining slowly. Today tourism is Dawson City's main industry, and gold-rush fever is recreated for a few weeks every summer.

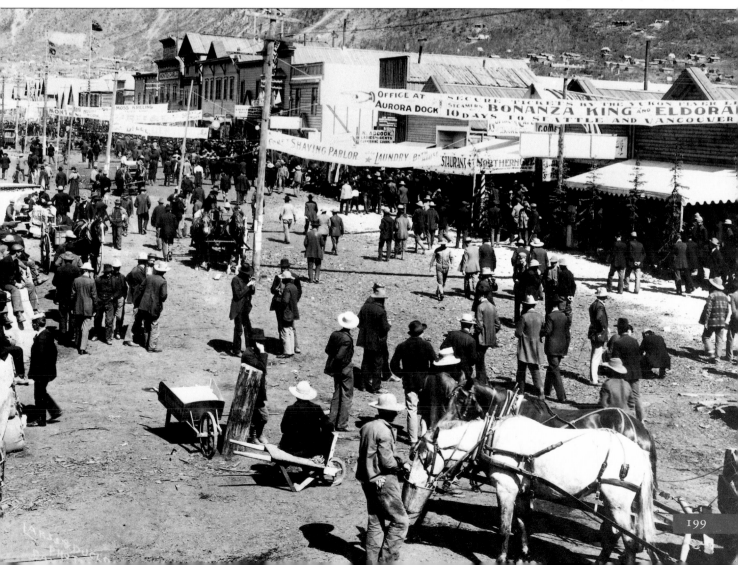

Dawson City in its heyday, 1899.

MINERS

A handful of miners still pan Yukon streams to gather a few grams of placer gold – the kind that can be found by carefully inspecting panfuls of river-washed sand and gravel. But the mines on which Yukon depends are big industrial operations employing the latest technology and hundreds of skilled and unionized miners. The prosperity of Yukon rises and falls with the price of precious metals. A single mine closing can be a disaster, and a single opening can spark a boom.

GEOPHYSICISTS

Today most prospecting is done by professional geologists and geophysicists. They analyze satellite maps, ponder electromagnetic surveys, and commission elaborate laboratory tests in their search for new ore bodies. Yet some of the great mineral discoveries still come from a lucky or careful inspection out on the land itself. To have much chance of making that lucky strike, however, you need lots of scientific preparation.

COMMUNITY LEADERS

Native peoples are a minority of all Yukoners (which is a different situation from that in the Northwest Territories and Nunavut), and Canadians of European descent predominate in Whitehorse and the mining towns of the territory. But in "the communities," Kutchin and Tutchone peoples still hunt and trap, and they seek to maintain control over the lands that provide for them. Leaders of the community not only give local guidance but also negotiate with the territorial government and with Ottawa. Their ultimate goal is a comprehensive land and government treaty that will secure Native rights into the future.

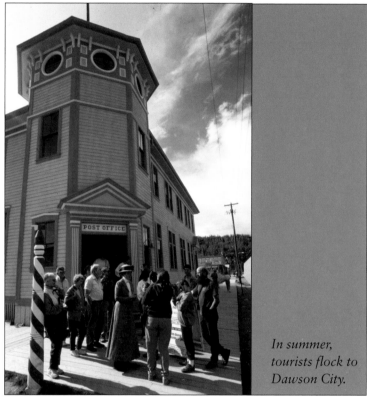

In summer, tourists flock to Dawson City.

TOURIST OPERATORS

Half a million visitors come to Yukon every summer, outnumbering the permanent residents by more than ten to one. Many come along the Alaska Highway and stop at Dawson City. Dawson is almost a ghost town in winter, but in summer, it recreates the Klondike of 1898. Parks Canada preserves many of the original gold-rush buildings and sites, and entertainers amuse visitors in the theatre and dance halls.

FARMERS

Farmers in Yukon? Well, yes, there are farmers in Yukon. As the territory's road and air links to the rest of the world improve, it becomes harder for northern farmers to compete. But there is always a market for fresh fruits and vegetables and for organic, locally grown produce. A few hardy producers still farm for their own subsistence or for sale to markets in Whitehorse.

At the height of the Yukon gold rush, Dawson City was the largest city west of Winnipeg. Today it is a village.

PIERRE BERTON (1920-)

Pierre Berton built his brilliant career as a journalist and writer in Vancouver and Toronto, but he grew up in Dawson City, son of a Trail of '98 miner. His pioneering history *Klondike* helped re-establish the North, the Klondike, and the gold rush in Canadian memory. Today the Berton home in Dawson is preserved as a writers' retreat.

MARTHA BLACK (1866-1957)

The Chicago socialite Martha Munger headed off for a temporary taste of the excitement of the Klondike gold rush in 1898. She stayed in Yukon and married George Black, who became commissioner of the territory and then a member of the Canadian Parliament. When he died, Martha, by then seventy, ran to take his place – and became just the second woman ever to sit in Canada's House of Commons.

GEORGE CARMACK (?-1922)

George Carmack had been around the Yukon River for years, and he was not very interested in gold. He preferred fishing and trapping with his Tagish wife, Shaaw Tlaa (Kate), and her brothers. Prospectors said he had "gone native." But in August 1896, he and his brothers-in-law did a little panning up Rabbit Creek. Suddenly they were millionaires, and the Klondike gold rush was under way.

FRANCIS FITZGERALD (1869-1911)

Insp. Francis Fitzgerald of the Royal North-West Mounted Police had been commanding the far northern outpost of Herschel Island for years, and he was a veteran Arctic traveller. In 1910, when he was chosen to represent the force at the coronation of King George V in London, he set off from Herschel Island with a small team, hoping to reach Dawson City in record time. But things went wrong. Fitzgerald lost his way, food ran low, and winter closed in around them. The Mounties launched a massive search for their "lost patrol," but Fitzgerald and all his men died in the snows in February 1911.

ROBERT SERVICE (1874-1958)

He was a bank clerk, not a gold miner. But he was a poet too, and during the Klondike gold fever, he found his subject – though the bank did not send him to Dawson City until 1904, after the rush was over. His

RNWMP officers prepare to leave Dawson in search of Francis Fitzgerald and his "lost patrol."

book *Songs of a Sourdough* became world famous, and his lively rhymes about the cremation of Sam McGee and the shooting of Dan McGrew have been popular ever since.

SAMUEL STEELE (1849-1919)

A soldier from England, barrel-chested and enormously strong, Sam Steele joined the new North-West Mounted Police in 1873. By 1885, he was in charge of the police detachments patrolling the new CPR line. In 1898, he found one of his greatest challenges: keeping order among tens of thousands of unruly goldseekers during the Klondike gold rush. It was Steele and his men who insisted that no one could come over the Chilkoot Pass without bringing a year's worth of supplies with them, and it was Steele's police who maintained the law in the goldfields themselves. Steele went on to lead Canadian troops in South Africa and during the First World War. Mount Steele, one of Yukon's highest mountains, is named for him.

Lt.-Col. Sam Steele, 1900.

Whitehorse is home to the Government Administration Building.

The name Yukon comes from the territory's great river, which is Yukunah to the Gwich'in people. Yukon became a territory separate from the North-West Territories in 1898. From 1898 until 1979, a commissioner reporting to Ottawa ran the Yukon government, but the members of his council were Yukoners, and after the 1950s, they were mostly elected (instead of appointed). In 1979, Yukoners took charge of their own internal affairs.

The Yukon government is now headed by a premier and a Cabinet, as in all the provinces. The government must command the support of a majority of the legislature of seventeen men and women, known as members of the Legislative Assembly (MLAs). Yukon is the only territory where political parties function much as they do in the provinces of Canada.

As a territory, Yukon does not have full control of its land or natural resources, but it now administers most of its own internal affairs. With barely thirty thousand people, Yukon must still look to the Canadian government for financial support.

The Yukon legislature meets in the Yukon Government Administration Building, designed by the architect Donovan Reeves and built in 1975–76.

NATIVE SELF-GOVERNMENT IN YUKON

Canada never signed any treaties with the peoples of Yukon. In the 1970s, the complaints of Gwich'in elders about encroachment by oil-exploration teams on their hunting territories helped to launch negotiations for the first comprehensive land and self-government treaties for Yukon. An umbrella agreement was reached in 1993, though many local details still remain to be settled. Since then, several land claims have been resolved.

The Council of Yukon First Nations represents the aboriginal peoples of Yukon in their treaty negotiations with the territorial government. All the Native communities of Yukon together elect a grand chief to lead the council.

Of course, land claims are not the only issue First Nations governments are addressing. Oil-and-gas exploration is going on and may one day be a vital source of wealth and employment in the territory. The Council of Yukon First Nations and the territorial government work together to ensure that both of them apply the same rules to exploration.

Today the First Nations people are no longer a majority in the territory, and Native culture has changed a great deal in the century since the gold rush. But the northern way of life is still strong in the Native communities, and the people who live there intend to continue to assert their rights and preserve their unique identity.

JOINED CONFEDERATION:
Formed out of the North-West Territories on June 13, 1898

TERRITORIAL FLOWER:
Fireweed

AREA:
482,500 square kilometres (4.9 per cent of Canada)

HIGHEST POINT:
Mount Logan, 5,959 metres (Mount Logan is the highest point in Canada; Canada's second-highest peak, Mount St. Elias, stands nearby)

POPULATION:
28,674 (about 17 per cent First Nations, 2 per cent Métis, 1 per cent Inuit)

GROWTH RATE:
Down 6.8 per cent since 1976

CAPITAL:
Whitehorse

MAIN COMMUNITIES:
Whitehorse (21,405 in 2001), Dawson City (1,251), Watson Lake (912)

YUKON GOVERNMENT INFORMATION ON THE INTERNET:
www.gov.yk.ca

THE SPELL OF THE YUKON

A Canadian is someone who can recite some lines of Robert Service, like this excerpt from "The Spell of the Yukon." Service first went to the territory several years after the Klondike gold rush, and he arrived to work in a bank, not to seek gold. But his poems, with their driving rhymes and vivid images, told the whole world what this northern land was like.

I wanted the gold, and I sought it,
    I scrabbled and mucked like a slave.
Was it famine or scurvy – I fought it;
    I hurled my youth into a grave.
I wanted the gold, and I got it –
    Came out with a fortune last fall, –
Yet somehow life's not what I thought it,
    And somehow the gold isn't all.

No! There's the land. (Have you seen it?)
    It's the cussedest land that I know,
From the big, dizzy mountains that screen it
    To the deep, deathlike valleys below.
Some say God was tired when He made it;
    Some say it's a fine land to shun;
Maybe; but there's some as would trade it
    For no land on earth – and I'm one.

You come to get rich (damned good reason);
    You feel like an exile at first;
You hate it like hell for a season,
    And then you are worse than the worst.
It grips you like some kinds of sinning;
    It twists you from foe to a friend;
It seems it's been since the beginning;
    It seems it will be to the end.

There's a land where the mountains are nameless,
    And the rivers all run God knows where;
There are lives that are erring and aimless,
    And deaths that just hang by a hair;
There are hardships that nobody reckons;
    There are valleys unpeopled and still;
There's a land – oh, it beckons and beckons,
    And I want to go back – and I will.

They're making my money diminish;
    I'm sick of the taste of champagne.
Thank God! when I'm skinned to a finish
    I'll pike to the Yukon again.
I'll fight – and you bet it's no sham-fight;
    It's hell! – but I've been there before;
And it's better than this by a damsite –
    So me for the Yukon once more.

There's gold, and it's haunting and haunting;
    It's luring me on as of old;
Yet it isn't the gold that I'm wanting
    So much as just finding the gold.
It's the great, big, broad land 'way up yonder,
    It's the forests where silence has lease;
It's the beauty that thrills me with wonder,
    It's the stillness that fills me with peace.

....

Most of the Northwest Territories is subarctic, rather than arctic, country. Most of it is south of the treeline, though the trees are mostly small and slow-growing. Its beauty is stark and simple. Plant life, animal life, and human life have always been thinly spread and precarious here. Yet the land we call the Northwest Territories has been home to the peoples of the Dene Nation for thousands of years. More recently, it has attracted European fur traders, miners, and adventurers, all of whom are drawn by the lure of one of the great wild land masses left on earth.

No part of Canada has changed its boundaries so much as the Northwest Territories has since it was first established as a territory in 1870. Today the NWT is part of a great political experiment. In 1999, the eastern and northern parts of the Northwest Territories became Nunavut, the homeland of the Inuit people. What remains of the big lonely land may, if its citizens decide in favour of it, become Denendeh, land of the Dene peoples.

The Northwest Territories is a place of contrasts. In Yellowknife, people live in a city much like those farther south, with tall buildings and streets full of cars. They have access to video stores, doctors' offices, coffee shops, sports facilities, and scheduled air service to Canada's other major cities. Many of these people are migrants who have come from somewhere else to work in the North, and most will probably move back south at some point in the future. But other people live in the thirty small communities "out on the land," where they have a lifestyle much more closely linked to the way their ancestors lived hundreds of years ago.

LANDSCAPES

From the Mackenzie Mountains on the Yukon border and across the muskeg and the boreal forest to the remote Arctic coast, the Northwest Territories extends over huge distances. Still, to appreciate the landscape there, it helps to admire small things. The Northwest Territories is home to thin forests, thin soils, and vegetation that shrinks down and shelters whenever it can. This is land that is still springing back after being pressed down by the weight of glacial ice ten thousand years ago. It is still covered with many thousands of lakes, with rock that has been ground down, and with fish and fur-bearing animals that were able to adapt to the change.

BOREAL FOREST

Much of the Northwest Territories is covered with a sparse forest of thin soils and stunted spruce, interspersed with rock outcroppings, lakes, and muskeg bogs. Geographers sometimes call this kind of country taiga (from a Russian word describing the stick-like trees) or boreal forest (*boreal* is a Latin term for "northern"). The Canadian boreal forest is a cold, dry, thin-soiled environment, easily damaged by human activity. The human population has always been thinly spread across it.

THE MACKENZIE DELTA

The Mackenzie River – Dehcho to the Dene people – is 4,491 kilometres long, making it Canada's longest river. At 1.8 million square kilometres, its drainage basin is the largest in Canada, and the river's tributary streams rise as far away as Jasper National Park, in the Alberta Rockies. Great Bear Lake and Great Slave Lake, both of which feed the Mackenzie, are the largest lakes entirely in Canada. From the headwaters in the Alberta and Yukon mountain ranges down to its vast delta on the Beaufort Sea in Alaska, the Mackenzie and its lowlands shape life throughout the western Arctic.

   The river has been a highway for trade and transport for thousands of years. Alexander Mackenzie travelled the length of the river in 1789, hoping to reach the Pacific. Today barges transport vital supplies to many riverbank communities throughout the summer and fall.

PINGOS

In the mostly flat Mackenzie Delta, draining water accumulates in places underneath the soil and swells up as it freezes. More water flows

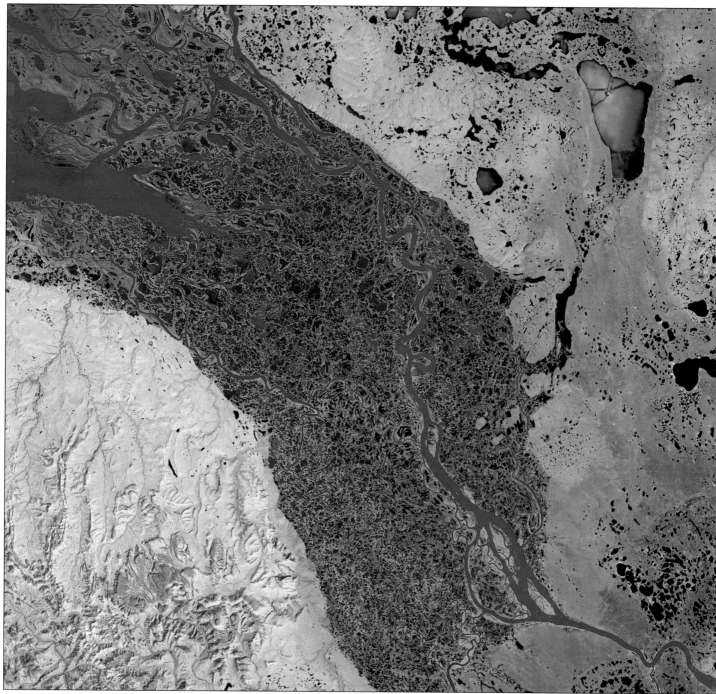

Satellite images like this one of the Mackenzie Delta allow scientists to chart vegetation growth and monitor spring ice breakup and flooding.

in, and the frozen bulge beneath the ground continues to expand. Gradually a smooth, rounded hill emerges from the flatlands of the river delta, often eventually growing to fifty or a hundred metres in height. These hills are called pingos, from an Inuit word, and the Mackenzie Delta has one of the world's most remarkable collections of them.

MOMENTS

1870 The North-West Territories (as the land was first called) came into being when Canada acquired the vast "territories" of the Hudson's Bay Company and additional lands "northwest" of what had been Canada. At this time, the North-West Territories extended north from the American border on the prairies and included northern Ontario and northern Quebec.

1880 Great Britain agreed to transfer to Canada all of the Arctic islands, which became part of the North-West Territories.

1905 When Alberta and Saskatchewan became provinces, the newly renamed Northwest Territories began to shrink to the regions north of sixty degrees north. An appointed council of civil servants, based in Ottawa, took over the governing of the territories.

1912 Quebec, Ontario, and Manitoba all expanded their boundaries, further reducing the size of the Northwest Territories.

1921 The first northern oilfield opened at Norman Wells. To ensure title to the Mackenzie valley, the Canadian government pushed through Treaty Eleven, the last of the so-called numbered treaties that transferred large tracts of land from the First Nations to Canada. The Dene Nation never accepted Treaty Eleven as legitimate, and negotiations for a new treaty have at last begun.

1922 Wood Buffalo National Park was created on the Alberta/NWT boundary. The park was established as a refuge for the last herd of wood bison and other endangered wildlife, including whooping cranes.

1933 A radium mine at Port Radium was one of the first mines in the Northwest Territories, launching what would become the territories' largest industry, mining. During the Second World War, radium and uranium from Port Radium were vital to the atomic-bomb project.

1951 The first election for members of the territorial council was held. However, the federal government still retained most of the power over the NWT.

1954 Canada and the United States agreed to co-operate in building the Distant Early Warning (DEW) Line, a network of northern radar bases designed to warn of any imminent missile attacks over the North Pole from the Soviet Union.

1967 The commissioner of the Northwest Territories and his civil service moved from Ottawa to the North. Yellowknife became the territorial capital.

1975 For the first time, all members of the territorial council of the Northwest Territories were elected by northern voters. Previously, some had been appointed by the Canadian government.

1975 The Indian Brotherhood of the Northwest Territories, the main political organization of Native peoples in the NWT, issued the Dene Declaration, a claim to land, political rights, and self-determination. Three years later, under President Mona Jacobs, the brotherhood renamed itself the Dene Nation.

1977 Judge Thomas Berger's royal commission report, *Northern Frontier, Northern Homeland*, recommended there be no further oil-pipeline development in the North until land claims were settled.

1984 Canada and the Inuvialuit of the Mackenzie Delta signed a comprehensive land-claims agreement for the Inuvialuit territory, the first of a series of agreements reached by Native groups in the territories.

1998 Canada's first diamond mine, the Ekati mine near Lac-de-Gras, started production. Diamonds were expected to become an important northern export.

1999 Nunavut became a separate territory, and the Northwest Territories, which still covered 24 per cent of the total area of Canada, considered its future.

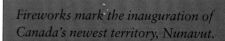

Fireworks mark the inauguration of Canada's newest territory, Nunavut.

Dene women and children prepare a moosehide in the early 1900s.

The Dene are great travellers. The Navajo people of the southern United States speak a language very similar to the Dene, and probably once lived in northern Canada.

DENE

Neighbours and fur-trading visitors called the peoples of what is today the Northwest Territories by several names: Chipewyan, Dogrib, Slavey, Hare. But they all spoke dialects of a language family known as Athapaskan, and mostly they called themselves Dene (the people). There were no large tribes or complex confederacies here. Because animals and resources were always thinly spread, family groups or small bands lived simply and covered a lot of ground every season, relying on their knowledge of the land to hunt woodland caribou, moose, and small game in the forests, and to catch fish in the lakes and streams. Sometimes the Dene peoples followed the caribou herds out on the Barren Grounds beyond the treeline.

INUVIALUIT

Many of the Inuit who lived in the Mackenzie Delta in the late nineteenth century died of diseases that whalers and traders brought. Into their land came newcomers from the west who spoke a language slightly different from the Inuktitut spoken by most of the Canadian Inuit. These people, the Inuvialuit, have remained somewhat separate from other Inuit groups. While an Inuit organization, the Inuit Tapirisat of Canada, worked for the creation of Nunavut, the Inuvialuit of the Mackenzie Delta and the western islands of the Beaufort Sea chose to remain part of the Northwest Territories, in partnership with the Dene Nation. The boundary between Nunavut and the Northwest Territories, which leaves the delta and some of the islands of the western Arctic in the Northwest Territories, respects their choice.

MÉTIS

Métis hunting and trading families followed the fur trade into the North in the 1800s, and Métis people soon settled in the southern part of the territory and along the Mackenzie Delta. Today the Métis are recognized by the government and the Dene as a separate group, and they have negotiated their own land claims and their own role in northern politics and daily life.

EURO-CANADIANS

Fur traders began venturing into the North in the late 1700s, and missionaries arrived in the late 1800s. Canadian government officials and the Royal Canadian Mounted Police came into the North early in the twentieth century. Around 1930, prospectors and miners began to settle in the North. In the 1950s, immigrants from "the South" begin to change Yellowknife and one or two other central places into cities that had streets, automobiles, office buildings, and other features of modern city life. Most immigrants to the North go for a temporary job with the government, in transportation, or in the mines, but many come to love the territory and the life there, and these transplants have chosen to make it their permanent home.

Members of this 1820 expedition led by Sir John Franklin were among the first Europeans to venture into what is now the Northwest Territories.

After Nunavut was created in 1999, non-Natives made up just over half of the population of the Northwest Territories. Treaties guarantee the Native nations lands and governing councils of their own, but non-Natives will play a large part in the future of the Northwest Territories.

BANNOCK

Bannock is the bread of the North. Trappers, prospectors, and hunters all have their own recipes, and these often use bacon grease or moose fat in place of margarine.

1 1/2 cups (375 mL) flour
1 tbsp (15 mL) baking powder
1/2 tbsp (5 mL) sugar
1/2 tsp (2 mL) salt
1/4 cup (50 mL) margarine or butter
1/2 cup (125 mL) water

Mix all the ingredients. If you are camping, place ingredients in a frying pan at the edge of the fire and cook about 20 minutes on each side. If you don't have a frying pan, twist the dough around a stick and hold it over the fire until it has risen and is crusty. At home, a 425°F (200°C) oven for 20 or 25 minutes will do the job.

Yellowknife is a modern city that still holds to traditional ways.

YELLOWKNIFE

Yellowknife, on the north shore of Great Slave Lake, is named for a Chipewyan band that lived in the area. However, the modern city of more than ten thousand people was founded by a gold rush. Mining began in 1934, and within two years, more than a thousand people had settled in the community. The mines still operate, but since 1967, Yellowknife has owed most of its growth to its role as the centre of government for the Northwest Territories. Yellowknife is the home of the territorial legislature, the Prince of Wales Northern Cultural Centre, and the Globe Theatre.

FORT SIMPSON

Fort Simpson is located in the southwestern part of the territories, on an island where the Liard River flows into the Mackenzie. A fur-trading post since the early 1800s, it is one of the oldest continuously occupied towns in the territories. In 1987, Pope John Paul II made a special trip to Fort Simpson to visit the many thousands of Dene who had come from all over the territories to meet him.

NORMAN WELLS

Northern oil wells? One day, the Beaufort Sea in the High Arctic may be one of Canada's great oil reserves. But since the 1940s, the town of Norman Wells has been pumping and refining oil from nearby deposits. In fact, for many years Norman Wells has produced more than a million barrels of oil annually. In 1985, a new pipeline was completed, and today much of Norman Wells's oil flows south to Alberta. Today the town has a population of about eight hundred people.

INUVIK

For a thousand years, the Inuit of the Mackenzie Delta lived in a community named Kittigazuit at the mouth of the main channel. Early in the twentieth century, Aklavik, which means "where there are bears" in Inuvialuit, became the main townsite of the region. But Aklavik is low-lying and prone to flooding. In the 1950s, the Canadian government began moving its people and buildings to higher ground, and a new town, called Inuvik (meaning "the place of people"), was born. Today Inuvik (home to the Igloo Church) and Tuktoyaktuk (on the seacoast) are the main settlements in the delta region. But not everyone left Aklavik when the government did. The Dene and Inuvialuit who remain say it is the town that would not die.

> Tuktoyaktuk, in the Mackenzie Delta, has the world's largest cluster of pingos, cone-shaped hills that rise up from the flat plain of the delta when ice swells underneath the surface.

HAY RIVER

Hay River, on the south shore of Great Slave Lake, has something unique in the territories: a railway. The rail link that connects it to northern Alberta makes it a transportation hub of the western Arctic. Mackenzie River barge traffic starts downriver from here, and the town of three thousand people is also a key waystation on the Mackenzie Highway, which heads north from Peace River, Alberta, all the way to Wrigley, on the Mackenzie River.

DIAMOND MINERS

Bits and pieces of smashed-up diamonds have been found in the soils that ancient glaciers carried south and then dumped across North America. Mining experts knew there had to be a source, a "diamond pipe," somewhere in the North. Gradually, they focused their attention on the rugged landscapes north of Yellowknife. Workers from Diamet Resources hit paydirt when they located a diamond pipe under Lac-de-Gras in 1998. But the diamond rush was never like an old-fashioned gold rush, where simple equipment could make any prospector rich. It takes millions of dollars and tons of elaborate machinery to gather diamonds that are buried deep in the northern rock, often beneath glacial lakes.

Ice roads keep northern centres open to supplies in the wintertime, but they can be hazardous for drivers.

ICE ROAD TRUCK DRIVERS

In some parts of the North, road transport comes to life in the winter. Ice roads run right across the boreal forest, doing less damage to the frozen ground than they would in summer, when the ground is soft and the plants are blossoming. With the lakes, streams, and muskeg (northern boggy ground) frozen solid, there is no need for bridges. In the springtime, however, truck drivers must keep an eye out for sudden thaws.

COMMUNITY LEADERS

Most of the Native peoples of the Northwest Territories live in about thirty small communities spread out across the vast expanse of the northern Arctic and subarctic. As these communities adapt to a rapidly changing world, they bring forth leaders who are at home in both traditional culture and modern society and politics. Young Native men and women who show leadership potential can rapidly become leaders in their communities, and many move on to represent those communities in First Nations organizations or in the territorial legislature in Yellowknife.

ABORIGINAL BROADCASTERS

In the 1970s, when the Canadian satellite *Anik* began sending broadcasting signals down to northern communities, almost all the radio and television programs originated in southern Canada. Today northern television and radio stations broadcast in more than a dozen aboriginal languages. The audiences may be small, but they are loyal. These stations have become a vital source of information and community-building for the First Nations of the Northwest Territories. Most of the broadcasters and a growing number of the producers and technicians are aboriginals.

TRAPPERS

Many Dene families hunt for food, and some keep traplines. Trapping is no longer the large industry it was in the heyday of the Hudson's Bay Company, when fur traders and missionaries were the only Europeans the people of the North ever saw. But for many Dene, living off the land and its animals is still commonplace.

NELLIE COURNOYEA (1940-   )

Nellie Cournoyea was born in Aklavik and grew up hunting and travelling with her Inuvialuit people. After working in radio, she helped found an Inuvialuit political organization and was elected to the Northwest Territories legislature. In 1991, the legislature chose her to be the government leader, and she played an active role in negotiating the division of Nunavut and the Northwest Territories. She seemed to have a brilliant political career ahead, but after one term in office, she chose to return to private life.

GEORGES ERASMUS (1948-   )

Georges Erasmus was born at Fort Rae, on Great Slave Lake, in 1948. As Dene life changed rapidly from its traditional ways, young people were thrust into leadership roles. Erasmus was elected president of the Dene Nation when he was still in his twenties. He went on to become national chief of the Assembly of First Nations, and he spoke for Native peoples during the constitutional battles of the 1980s. In the 1990s, when the Canadian government created the Royal Commission on Aboriginal Affairs, Erasmus was chosen to direct it.

SIR JOHN FRANKLIN (1786-1847)

The British naval officer Sir John Franklin is famous for having died with all of his 146 men trying to find the Northwest Passage. But before that, he had led two expeditions through what is now the Northwest Territories. He mapped the Mackenzie and Coppermine rivers and a long stretch of the Arctic coast. If he had not died so spectacularly, trapped in the ice with two naval ships, he might be remembered as a very successful overland surveyor of northern Canada.

STUART HODGSON (1924-   )

Commissioners of the Northwest Territories had always been civil servants based in Ottawa. But when Stuart Hodgson, a labour leader and naval veteran from Vancouver, became commissioner in 1967, he changed the way things were done. Hodgson moved his office to Yellowknife, and he travelled constantly throughout the North. He delegated more things to his elected councillors, and he began preparing to transfer control of the government to northerners.

Frozen bodies of crew members of the Franklin expedition gave clues to the fate of the doomed explorers.

ALBERT JOHNSON (?-1932)

In December 1931, for no reason anyone ever discovered, a trapper who called himself Albert Johnson shot a Royal Canadian Mounted Police officer who was checking traplines in the Northwest Territories. The chase was on, but the Mounties soon discovered that Johnson's woodcraft was brilliant. In winter darkness, across 240 kilometres of the territories and into Yukon, they pursued him, even bringing in the pioneer bush pilot Wop May to find his trail. Finally, after forty-eight days, with another Mountie dead and one wounded, the force caught up to the so-called Mad Trapper on Rat River, in northern Yukon, and shot him dead in a gunfight. No one ever learned who Albert Johnson was – or how he had become so skilled at survival on the run.

ALEXANDER MACKENZIE (1764-1820)

Alexander Mackenzie was a partner in the fur-trading North West Company from Montreal (rival of the Hudson's Bay Company), and he wanted to open up a canoe route all the way from Montreal to the Pacific. When he set off from Lake Athabaska (in what is now northern Alberta) in 1789, he soon found that the river he was following ran north, not west. Mackenzie named this river, which the local people called Dehcho, the River of Disappointment, but he followed it all the way to the Arctic Ocean. Soon traders had built a chain of posts along the river, and they named it after Mackenzie. Meanwhile, he found another route across the mountains and reached the Pacific in 1793.

Alexander Mackenzie was the first European to chart the river that now bears his name.

MATONABBEE (1737-1782)

The Hudson's Bay Company wanted Samuel Hearne to survey the interior of the continent, but none of his expeditions got very far. Then, in 1770, he met Matonabbee and attached himself to his Chipewyan family. They travelled together as the Chipewyan did, feasting when game was plentiful, starving when it was scarce, moving when they could. Matonabbee took Hearne to the Arctic Ocean, and they looked for copper mines along the Coppermine River. They went on to Great Slave Lake and then back to Prince of Wales's Fort, on Hudson Bay. The thirty-two-month walk made Samuel Hearne a famous explorer among Europeans, and he always said it was Matonabbee who had made it possible.

LAW AND ORDER

The territorial legislature in Yellowknife resembles a zinc-clad snow house.

The Northwest Territories is represented in the House of Commons by one member of Parliament, and it shares one senator with Nunavut. For territorial politics, however, the Northwest Territories has evolved one of the most original and interesting political systems in Canada.

There are no political parties in Northwest Territories elections. After being elected, the fourteen individual members decide among themselves which members will form the government and who will act as government leader. This government remains in power as long as it retains the support of a majority of the members or until the five-year term of the legislature expires, whichever comes first. This style of governance has a long history in the Northwest Territories. Traditionally, aboriginal communities have governed themselves by consensus, and the territorial government respects that tradition. To encourage consensus, the legislative chamber in Yellowknife is even arranged in a circle, instead of having sets of government and opposition benches placed across from each other.

Since the 1960s, more and more responsibility for territorial affairs has passed from Ottawa to the territorial government. The head of government, the territorial commissioner, used to be a powerful official as Ottawa's representative in the North, but today he or she acts primarily as a ceremonial figure, like a provincial lieutenant-governor. Native members hold many of the seats in the territorial legislature. Since the 1990s, several First Nations politicians have held the offices of government leader and territorial commissioner.

The legislative assembly of the Northwest Territories was opened in 1993. It overlooks Frame Lake in Yellowknife and is sheathed in reflective zinc panels made from minerals mined in the territory.

NATIVE SELF-GOVERNMENT IN THE NORTHWEST TERRITORIES

Until 1960, Native peoples did not have the right to vote in Canadian elections. Today the Dene, Métis, and Inuvialuit play a large role in territorial politics, though Native peoples are no longer a majority in the Northwest Territories.

During the 1980s and 1990s, the main First Nations groups of the Northwest Territories worked to negotiate land claims with the government of Canada. These agreements were to confirm their permanent ownership and control of large tracts in the territory. The Inuvialuit land-claim agreement was the first to be completed and signed (in 1984). It was followed by Dene and Métis agreements in 1994.

Today the Northwest Territories is the only province or territory in Canada with its own official languages commissioner. It needs one! The official languages of the Northwest Territories are Chipewyan, Cree, Dogrib, Gwich'in, English, French, three forms of Inuktitut, and two forms of Slavey – eleven languages altogether. Each aboriginal language has its part of the territory where it is most common, but many people speak more than one.

Each of these languages is used in the legislature of the Northwest Territories. People there can expect to be served by their government in whichever language they prefer to use.

JOINED CONFEDERATION:
July 13, 1870

TERRITORIAL FLOWER:
Mountain avens

AREA:
1,299,000 square kilometres

HIGHEST POINT:
Mount Sir James MacBrien (2,762 metres above sea level)

POPULATION:
37,360 (about 52 per cent non-aboriginal; 28 per cent Dene, Cree, and other North American Indian; 10 per cent Inuvialuit and Inuit; 9 per cent Métis)

GROWTH RATE:
Down 5.8 per cent since 1996

CAPITAL:
Yellowknife

MAIN COMMUNITIES:
Yellowknife (16,541), Hay River (3,510), Inuvik (2,894), Fort Smith (2,441)

NORTHWEST TERRITORIES GOVERNMENT INFORMATION ON THE INTERNET:
www.gov.nt.ca

WRITING IN CREE

Ever written a letter in Cree? Probably not. But you could, if you had learned the unique Cree alphabet known as Cree syllabics.

The Cree people have always lived in the woodlands and along the shores of northern Canada, from Quebec west into the Prairie provinces. They are a hunting and fishing people, and for many thousands of years, their culture was oral. There were Cree orators and Cree poets, but no one wrote down the Cree language.

About 1840, James Evans was a missionary at Norway House in what is now Manitoba. He worked with Cree people to find ways to write symbols that matched the way they spoke. The result was Cree syllabics.

Syllabics do not use our familiar twenty-six-letter alphabet. Each of the thirty-six symbols used in Cree writing represents a syllable or sound made up of a vowel and a consonant together. There are four main vowel sounds used in spoken Cree, and therefore represented in Cree syllabics, and these correspond to the English vowels a, e, i, and o. The nine consonants represented in the language are ch, p, t, k, m, n, s, w, and y. Combining the nine consonant forms with the four vowel forms gives the thirty-six symbols that form the Cree alphabet.

Over more than a century and a half, syllabics have become part of Cree culture. Books and newspapers, as well as personal letters, have been written in Cree syllabics. Cree is one of the strongest aboriginal languages in Canada today. The Cree people are proud of having their own way of reflecting their unique culture in writing.

	W	P	T	K	CH	M	N	S	Y
A	◁·	<	⊂	b	∪	L	ₒ	˥	ϲ
E	▽·	V	∪	٩	∩	⊓	ᵓ	˥	ʕ
I	△·	∧	∩	ρ	⌐	⌐	σ	ʅ	ʌ
O	▷·	>	⊃	d	⌐	⌐	ₒ	ʅ	⊣

NUNAVUT

ALERT

ELLESMERE ISLAND
NATIONAL PARK

ELLESMERE
ISLAND

BAFFIN

RESOLUTE

LANCASTER SOUND

NANISIVIK

POND
INLET

BAFFIN ISLAND

VICTORIA
ISLAND

IGLOOLIK

IQALUKTUUTIAQ
(CAMBRIDGE BAY)

KUGLUKTUK   UMINGMAKTOK   UQSUQTUUQ (GJOA HAVEN)
(COPPERMINE)   (BAY CHIMO)
                                              MELVILLE
                                              PENINSULA

KINGAOK   NAUJAAT
(BATHURST INLET)   (REPULSE BAY)

                                                              KINGNA
                                                              (CAPE DOR

COPPERMINE RIVER

                                              SOUTHAMPTON
                                              ISLAND

QAMANITTUAQ
(BAKER LAKE)

                                        IGLULIGAARJUK
                                        (CHESTERFIELD INLET)

NORTHWEST
TERRITORIES   KANGIQLINIQ
                     (RANKIN INLET)

                ARVIAT
                (ESKIMO POINT)

                                        HUDSON BAY

GREENLAND

DAVIS STRAIT

QIKIQTARJUAK
(BROUGHTON ISLAND)

JITTUQ
ONAL PARK

IQALUIT

HUDSON BAY

SON STRAIT

ALL
ISLANDS IN
HUDSON BAY
BELONG TO
NUNAVUT

UEBEC

Nunavut means "our land" in Inuktitut, the language of the Inuit people. Since April 1999, Nunavut has been the thirteenth and newest Canadian territory, the only part of Canada where aboriginal people form the majority of citizens and voters.

Nunavut is the true Arctic, the far northern land beyond the treeline, home of the Barren Ground caribou, the muskox, the polar bear, and the narwhal. Nunavut is also the home of most of the Canadian Inuit, the twenty-five thousand people of the Arctic coasts and islands. Nunavut extends from the interior Barrens west of Hudson Bay to the Arctic islands, where the dramatic search for the Northwest Passage was played out, and as far north as the distant reaches of Ellesmere Island, just seven hundred kilometres from the North Pole.

A century ago, only a few whalers, missionaries, and traders ventured into Nunavut from the outside world. During the twentieth century, government administrators, missionaries, and prospectors became much more common across the North. Today Nunavut is also a tourist destination for adventurous hikers, climbers, and even cruise-ship passengers. But most of all, Nunavut remains the land of the Inuit and the place where they will work out their future and preserve their past.

LANDSCAPES

T he Nunavut landscape includes great mountains, flowing glaciers, spectacular icebergs, and herds of prehistoric-looking muskoxen. Sometimes the only vegetation visible will be a brief blossoming of wildflowers or colourful lichens on the bare rock. And animal life will often be absolutely invisible to anyone but an Inuit hunter whose eye has been trained to spot the tell-tale signs of prey. But for those who know how to look, the lands and waters of Nunavut provide many diverse habitats and truly breathtaking vistas.

Auyuittuq was Canada's first national park north of the Arctic Circle.

EASTERN ARCTIC

Ellesmere, Devon, and Baffin, the islands facing Greenland in the eastern Arctic, are spectacularly rugged and mountainous. Peaks as much as two thousand metres tall rise almost vertically from saltwater fjords, and glaciers flow down steep-sided valleys to tide-water. Narwhals, beluga whales, seals, polar bears, and seabirds thrive in or near the coastal waters. Hares, foxes, lemmings, and weasels find homes amid the sparse vegetation of the interior. Arctic flowers blossom in the meadows during the endless sunshine of the brief summer, but much of the land is ice-covered all year.

To preserve some of this fragile, spectacular environment, Canada created the first Arctic national park, Auyuittuq, in 1972. In 1988, Ellesmere Island National Park became the world's most northerly national park.

THE BARRENS

There is a reason why the boundary between Nunavut and the Northwest Territories zigzags diagonally across the northern mainland of Canada. The boundary follows the treeline, and the treeline is both a natural and a cultural dividing line. Southwest of the line is Dene territory; northeast of it is Inuit country.

Most Inuit have been people of the sea ice and the coastline, but the rugged, rocky Barrens are home to vast migrating herds of caribou, and some Inuit bands came inland to hunt them, usually ambushing the herds at river crossings or lake narrows. The community of Baker Lake, on a tidal inlet that reaches deep into the Barren Lands, is the only inland town in Nunavut.

ARCTIC ARCHIPELAGO

An archipelago is a group of islands, and the Arctic islands that stretch from the northern mainland of Canada towards the North Pole form the largest archipelago in the world. In winter, the snowy surfaces of these low, flat islands of the western Arctic blend almost invisibly into the frozen sea channels around them.

The sea ice was the most important place in the western Arctic. Under the ice, the water teemed with rich marine life upon which both polar bears and Inuit hunting bands depended. When the explorer and anthropologist Vilhjalmur Stefansson realized how the Inuit could live on the apparently barren icy wastes, he called the High Arctic "the friendly Arctic."

THE NORTHWEST PASSAGE

Almost as soon as Ferdinand Magellan, a Portuguese explorer in the service of Spain, discovered a "southwest passage" leading to Asia at the southern tip of South America, European sailors started looking for a "north-west passage" over the top of North America. By 1800, it was certain that any route through the Arctic islands would be too ice-choked ever to be useful for trade. Nevertheless, explorers and adventurers continued to seek a way through them. Sir John Franklin's 1845 expedition, which became trapped in ice and was lost with all hands, was one of Britain's great naval disasters. Roald Amundsen finally succeeded in completing the journey in 1906, though it took him three years. In the late twentieth century, icebreakers and oil tankers, and even some cruise ships, have sailed between the Atlantic and the Pacific in a single season, but the fabled Northwest Passage will never be a commercial shipping route.

Roald Amundsen, here incorrectly identified as "Raoul" Amundsen, is pictured in the year he completed his heroic journey.

CAPTAIN RAOUL AMUNDSEN, DISCOVERER OF NORTH WEST PASSAGE.

MOMENTS

1880   Britain transferred the High Arctic islands to Canada, which added them to its North-West Territories without consulting the Inuit peoples to whom the land really belonged.

1902   After whalers, missionaries, traders, and officials came to live in the North, tuberculosis and other diseases ripped through Inuit populations with terrible effects. In 1902, a brief epidemic killed all the Sadlermiut Inuit of Southampton Island, at the western end of Hudson Strait.

1906   The Norwegian adventurer Roald Amundsen and his vessel *Gjoa* reached the Alaskan coast and the Pacific Ocean, completing the first journey through the Northwest Passage by ship.

1909   The American Robert Peary proclaimed himself the first person to reach the North Pole. He denounced Frederick Cook, a rival explorer who also claimed to have reached the pole, as a fraud. Today some doubts remain about Peary's navigation and whether he actually made it as far as he claimed.

1913   Vilhjalmur Stefansson surveyed the western Arctic islands. When he mapped their northwestern edges, he added the last substantial piece of unsurveyed coastline to the map of the world.

1929   Uluksak, an Inuk from Coppermine, had been in a Canadian jail in Alberta since his conviction for killing a missionary in 1913. When he became ill with tuberculosis, Canada sent Uluksak home to die. In the few more months he lived, he spread his tuberculosis to his relatives. A terrible epidemic was born that would kill half the Coppermine Inuit.

1939   A Canadian court ruled that relations with the Inuit were a federal responsibility, setting the stage for future negotiations between Canada and the Arctic peoples. The Inuit had never been subject to Canada's Indian Act, and they had made no treaties with Canada.

1942   Capt. Henry Larsen piloted the RCMP vessel *St. Roch* through the Northwest Passage from east to west. To the Inuit, he

Robert Peary on the deck of the steamship Roosevelt, *the vessel from which he launched his assault on the North Pole.*

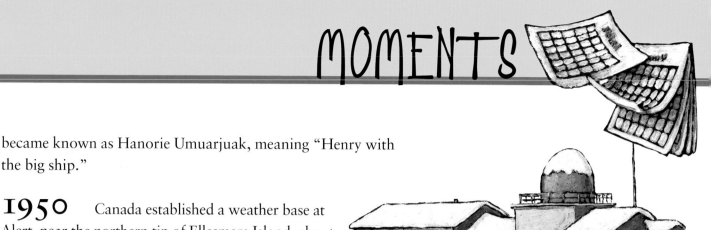

became known as Hanorie Umuarjuak, meaning "Henry with the big ship."

1950 Canada established a weather base at Alert, near the northern tip of Ellesmere Island, about as close to the North Pole as one can get by land. Alert soon became a year-round military base.

1953 Canada wanted to demonstrate to the world that the High Arctic was Canadian. To build up the population in the Far North, the government relocated Inuit families from northern Quebec to Cornwallis Island, where a weather base had recently been established. They led a grim, difficult life in a new environment they knew little about, and Canada later admitted it had treated them very badly.

1960 The artist and civil servant James Houston gave the Inuit of Cape Dorset, on Baffin Island, lessons in printmaking techniques, and they quickly won international recognition and commercial success for their brilliant and imaginative work. Inuit art has been admired and collected worldwide ever since.

1969 With the help of Canadian icebreakers, the American supertanker *Manhattan* passed through the Northwest Passage. Despite its success, most observers remained convinced that the passage was neither practical nor environmentally sensible as an oil-tanker route.

1971 The Inuit and Inuvialuit peoples founded the Inuit Tapirisat of Canada, to give them a united voice in dealing with Canada and preserving their culture. All adult Inuit can vote for the leadership of the Inuit Tapirisat.

1972 Canada created Auyuittuq National Park, the first of several Arctic nature and wildlife preserves.

1982 Voters in the Northwest Territories narrowly approved the creation of a new territory covering the Inuit homelands.

1999 Nunavut, Canada's new territory, was founded in April.

PEOPLES

INUIT

About a thousand years ago, the northern climate warmed for a few centuries. From Alaska, the ancestors of today's Inuit moved swiftly in skin boats called umiaks through the opening channels of the Arctic archipelago. They settled all the territories in which the Inuit now live, from the Mackenzie Delta to Labrador. When the climate later cooled, the Inuit had the skills and the tools to adapt to changing conditions.

The Inuit survive in one of the world's harshest, coldest, least fertile environments. They are a remarkable example of human adaptability to difficult and unlikely conditions. In the second half of the twentieth century, most Inuit gave up the hard and dangerous migratory life and began settling in a small number of communities, close to medical care, schooling, and other modern services. The Canadian government strongly encouraged them to settle in this way. Today the children of migratory hunting families may travel by jet, communicate by the Internet, acquire university degrees, and run modern businesses.

The Inuit still hope to retain their relationship with the land, even when most now live in towns. The culture of Canada and the world arrives in their stores and through their televisions, and after centuries of self-reliance, they find themselves a small minority in Canadian society. Inuit communities struggle with unemployment, despair, substance abuse, and suicide. Yet the Inuit have also produced a remarkable generation of young leaders to respond to these problems.

Nunavut is the heartland of the Canadian Inuit, but not all Inuit live there. There are also Inuit communities in Labrador, Quebec, and the Northwest Territories. About 25,000 of the 150,000 Inuit peoples of the world live in Canada, and about 18,000 of those live in Nunavut.

WHALERS

European whalers began hunting in Davis Strait in the 1600s. By the 1800s, they were catching a thousand whales a year. In the early twentieth century, whalers pushed deeper into the Arctic. They began

> You could actually keep quite warm in a snow house. The entrance tunnel, which was dug down deeper than the living area, acted as a "cold trap," while a small lamp warmed the interior.

wintering over, often employing Inuit as pilots, hunters, and crew. The impact on Inuit society was great. Diseases spread, but so did European goods, and many Inuit today have British, American, or Scandinavian whalers among their ancestors.

The invasion of European and American whalers also pushed Canada to establish its control over the North. RCMP stations began to be opened across the islands of the Arctic archipelago after 1903.

The whaling industry was at its peak around the middle of the 1800s.

SOUTHERNERS

The Inuit remain the majority in Nunavut, but the North has always attracted small numbers of southern Canadians and others. Some are doctors, government administrators, construction workers, or teachers who come for a few exciting and well-paid years in the Far North before returning home. But Nunavut has also always lured people who fall in love with the northern people and the northern landscape and never want to live anywhere else again.

CARIBOU CHILI

Caribou meat, although rarely eaten elsewhere in Canada, is a staple of the Inuit diet. This spicy chili recipe puts a southern spin on this northern favourite.

4 lbs (1.5 kg) caribou meat, chunked or ground
1 large onion, chopped
2 cloves garlic, minced
1 tsp (5 mL) oregano

2 tsp (10 mL) cumin
1 cup (250 mL) red wine or beef broth
2 tbsp (30 mL) chili powder
1 small can tomato paste
1/2 tsp (2 mL) cayenne pepper
salt to taste

Place meat, onion, and garlic in a large heavy skillet and cook until light coloured. Add oregano, cumin, wine or broth, chili powder, tomato paste, cayenne pepper sauce, and salt. Bring mixture to a boil, then lower heat and simmer for one hour. If possible, allow chili to cool and sit for at least 6 hours before reheating and serving.

Iqaluit is more like a small Canadian city than most Nunavut communities.

IQALUIT (FROBISHER BAY)

Iqaluit, near the site of a South Baffin Inuit fishing camp, became an air base in 1942 and a DEW Line supply base in 1952. Under the name Frobisher Bay, it gradually became the administrative centre of the eastern Arctic. The town's name was changed back to Iqaluit (place of fish) in 1987, and it was the logical choice for the capital of the new territory of Nunavut. More than any other Arctic community, Iqaluit resembles a modern southern city, with cars, an airport, high-rise buildings – and also poverty and crime.

NANISIVIK

Nanisivik, near the northern end of Baffin Island, has little wildlife and was never an important Inuit settlement, but it does have rich deposits of cadmium, lead, silver, and zinc. In 1974, the buildings and machinery of a mine were barged to the area, unloaded, and assembled. Nanisivik has been one of the world's most northerly mines ever since.

QAMANITTUAQ (BAKER LAKE)

Of Nunavut's twenty-eight permanent communities, Baker Lake is the only one that is not on the seacoast. It began as a gathering place for the Caribou Inuit of the Barren Grounds. Its Inuit name, Qamanittuaq, reasonably enough, means "far inland." Many of the people still hunt and fish for their living, and the carvers of Baker Lake are well known. Though the rest of Canada thinks of Nunavut as being far to the north, Baker Lake actually lies close to the geographical centre of the country.

KUGLUKTUK (COPPERMINE)

Rumours that the people of the central Arctic coast owned rich stores of copper inspired many explorations to the Coppermine River, including that of Samuel Hearne and Matonabbee in 1780. Coppermine, at the mouth of the river, became a trading post and mission centre in 1916. Today it is one of the communities of the Copper Inuit on

Coronation Gulf. It recently returned to the Inuktitut name Kugluktuk (place of rapids). The copper that made it famous for so long has turned out to be scarce, and so far, it has not been worth mining. Many of the Native peoples still follow a way of life based on hunting and fishing. The islands north of Kugluktuk support large herds of muskoxen.

IGLOOLIK

Igloolik (place of the houses) stands beside a narrow strait between Baffin Island and the mainland. The strait abounds in seals and walruses, and the community appears to have been continuously occupied for some four thousand years. The Dorset and Paleoeskimo peoples, who inhabited the Arctic in earlier periods, lived around Igloolik, and ancestors of the modern Igloolik Inuit settled in this area a thousand years ago. Many archeologists have come to examine the remains of earlier times at Igloolik, and anthropologists come here to study modern Inuit culture and society. An international biological station opened at Igloolik in 1972.

LANCASTER SOUND

This broad channel, four hundred kilometres long and one hundred kilometres wide, lies between Baffin Island and Devon Island. It is the main entrance to the Northwest Passage. It is also one of the Arctic archipelago's largest, most important polynyas. A polynya is a stretch of Arctic water where wind and currents prevent a complete freeze-over, even in winter. The open water attracts sea life, particularly the sea mammals that cannot survive without air. Lancaster Sound is one of the richest biological zones in the Arctic; it supports millions of birds, as well as whales, walruses, and polar bears in large numbers.

HUNTERS

Most Canadians find it hard to imagine eating the raw marrow of a caribou thigh bone or the oily fat from a whale. But Inuit people thrived on such foods for thousands of years. Many of them continue to hunt and fish for their food today. They worry that the younger Inuit who work in towns and buy packaged food from stores will lose the traditional skills – and perhaps their Inuit identity as well.

THE FORCES AT ALERT

One of the most remote places of the world, Alert stands near the northern tip of Ellesmere Island, little more than seven hundred kilometres from the North Pole. Members of the Canadian forces live and work there year-round, in the world's most northerly permanent settlement. (What do they do? Most of it is secret.) When a military supply plane crashed near Alert in October 1991, killing five, much of Canada followed the news anxiously as search-and-rescue technicians from the Canadian forces parachuted into a storm to rescue the thirteen survivors.

Inuit and other aboriginal peoples from around the polar region gather every few years to play traditional Inuit sports in the Arctic Winter Games.

COMMUNITY NURSE PRACTITIONERS

The Inuit always knew that people who became sick or injured out on the land would probably die. For most Nunavut Inuit, the ability to get medical services, as well as education, helped persuade them to give up an old life based on migrating across the land and the ice in small bands. Today most Nunavut communities have a hospital tended by nurse practitioners rather than doctors. Local hospitals rely on their

Evacuation flights like this one have become less common thanks to the efforts of nurse practitioners.

own knowledge, on radio and computer links to centres like Iqaluit, and on medical evacuation flights for emergencies. More and more of the nurse practitioners are Inuit men and women, trained at Nunavut's own Arctic College in Iqaluit.

ARTISTS

If you walk through Cape Dorset or Lake Harbour or Gjoa Haven, you will probably see a young man sitting outside his door, with chisels and power tools, patiently transforming a piece of local stone into a unique and evocative carving. At the community hall, a group of women may be preparing colourful prints or carefully sewing spectacular garments. In many Nunavut communities, a career as an artist is almost as common as one in teaching, hunting, or nursing.

SUSAN AGLUKARK (1967-   )

Susan Aglukark (Uuliniq is her Inuktitut name) grew up moving among the Inuit communities that her father served as a Pentecostal minister. When she was still a child, she began singing at home and in church. Her first album was released in 1991, and the second, *Arctic Rose,* was a hit in 1992.

JOHN AMAGOALIK (1948-   )

John Amagoalik was not born in what is now Nunavut. In 1953, he and his parents were among the Inuit families from northern Quebec who were sent to live under grim and difficult conditions at Resolute Bay, on Cornwallis Island, because the government wanted settlers there to strengthen Canadian sovereignty in the North. Amagoalik grew up to become a leader in Inuit political organization and an experienced negotiator on behalf of his people. From 1993 until 1999, he led the Nunavut Implementation Commission, which took charge of the creation of the new territory. For his years of hard work, Amagoalik has become known as "the Father of Nunavut."

JAMES HOUSTON (1921-   )

After studying art in his hometown of Toronto, James Houston went north as a Canadian civil servant in 1948. He was soon fascinated by the artistic talents of the Inuit people around Cape Dorset, on Baffin Island, and he became convinced that art collectors around the world would also admire them. With Houston's help, the artists of Cape Dorset learned the techniques of making fine-art prints. After several years of trial and error, Inuit art exploded onto the world stage. Houston, who had lived among the Inuit in the last days of their traditional migratory ways, went on to become a successful novelist and artist in his own right. Art prints and sculpture have made Cape Dorset famous all over the world.

KENOJUAK ASHEVAK (1927-   )

Kenojuak was born in a hunting camp on southern Baffin Island. In the 1950s, she was one of the first women to work in the printmaking studio that James Houston established at Cape Dorset. Her drawings and prints, mostly of birds, are crisply designed and brilliantly imaginative. They quickly became world-famous classics of the Cape Dorset print-

making style. Kenojuak's *Enchanted Owl* is one of the best-known Inuit print images. It appeared on a Canadian stamp in 1970.

PETER FREUCHEN ITTINUAR (1950-   )

Peter Ittinuar, whose grandfather was a Danish Arctic explorer, was raised at Chesterfield Inlet (now Igluligaarjuk), on Hudson Bay. He became an Inuktitut teacher and the director of the Inuit Tapirisat of Canada before running for the House of Commons in the northern riding of Nunutsiaq in 1979. His victory made him the first Inuk member of Parliament.

MICHAEL KUSUGAK (1948-   )

For his first six years, Michael Kusugak lived the nomadic hunting life of his Inuit people around Repulse Bay, on the Hudson Bay coast. Later he went to school in Saskatchewan. Back in Repulse Bay, he began telling traditional stories to his children. When the Canadian children's writer Robert Munsch visited the community, he helped Kusugak turn his stories into a series of best-selling children's books.

PETER PITSEOLAK (1902-1973)

Among the south Baffin Island Inuit, Peter Pitseolak was a leader who wanted to record the traditional life of his people. After meeting explorers and travellers in the North, he began taking photographs. By the 1940s, he had his own camera. He often developed his own prints in a hunting igloo. Pitseolak's photographs are a precious record of Inuit life, and he also drew and wrote about his experiences.

QITDLARSSUAQ (ABOUT 1825-1875)

A powerful shaman, Qitdlarssuaq had to flee from Baffin Island to escape vengeance after killing an enemy. In his dreams, he saw a lost group of Inuit living far to the north, and he decided to find them. Qitdlarssuaq led about fifty Inuit followers on a long migration across Devon and Ellesmere islands. Finally, they reached northern Greenland and the isolated Thule people, who had long since lost their knowledge of how to make and use kayaks and bows and arrows. However he had learned of the existence of Inuit kinfolk in that faraway land, Qitdlarssuaq brought them new skills that revived north Greenland Inuit culture. Sadly, he died on his way back to Baffin Island.

LAW AND ORDER

The Nunavut legislative assembly is Canada's newest legislature, built in 1999.

Nunavut is unique among Canadian provinces and territories, for it has a majority of aboriginal people in its population. Still, its government is similar to that of Yukon and the Northwest Territories. The official head of the territorial government is the commissioner, who is appointed by the Canadian government in Ottawa. Like a provincial lieutenant-governor, the commissioner leaves most decisions to a government answerable to the elected legislature.

As in the Northwest Territories, there are no parties in Nunavut elections. The government leader and the men and women who form the Cabinet must retain the support of a majority of the nineteen members of the legislature. Members are elected as individuals, not party representatives. The emphasis here, as in the Northwest Territories, is on governing by consensus, and once again the legislative chamber is arranged in a circle.

Nunavut's capital is Iqaluit, on Baffin Island. The new legislative building, designed by the Arcop Group and Keith Irving, opened in 1999, just in time for the founding of the new territory. Like other Iqaluit buildings, it was built without a foundation because of the permafrost. Its sleek blue-glass shell is designed to accommodate pre-vailing winds and snowdrifts.

There are three districts within Nunavut. Baffin Region covers the eastern islands. Keewatin Region covers the mainland west of Hudson Bay. Kitikmeot Region includes most of the western Arctic islands and the north coast of the mainland. Like the other northern territories, Nunavut is not financially self-supporting. It relies on financial support from the Canadian government.

NUNAVUT PLACE NAMES

Many of the communities of Nunavut have recently returned to their original names. Eskimo Point has become Arviat, meaning "bowhead whale." Broughton Inlet has become Qikiqtarjuak ("big island"). Others, like Cape Dorset and Pond Inlet, still use their European name but also have an Inuktitut name (Kingnait, meaning "mountains," for Cape Dorset, and Mittimatalik, "place of Mittima's grave," for Pond Inlet).

The legislative chamber, where members' seats are arranged in a circle.

JOINED CONFEDERATION:
April 1, 1999 (previously Nunavut was part of the Northwest Territories, first acquired by Canada in 1870)

TERRITORIAL FLOWER:
Purple saxifrage

AREA:
1,994,000 million square kilometres

HIGHEST POINT:
Mount Barbeau, Ellesmere Island (2,626 metres)

POPULATION:
26,745

GROWTH RATE:
8.1 per cent since 1996

CAPITAL:
Iqaluit

MAIN COMMUNITIES:
Iqaluit (5,236 in 2001), Rankin Inlet (2,177), Arviat (1,899), Cambridge Bay (1,309)

NUNAVUT GOVERNMENT INFORMATION ON THE INTERNET:
www.gov.nu.ca

WHAT DO INUKSUIT MEAN?

An Inuit stone marker, which you see up in the Arctic, is called an inuksuk, isn't it? Well, actually, one is an inuksuk, two are called inuksuuk, and three or more are inuksuit.

That's not the half of it. Here are a few of the names and types of inuksuit that Inuit hunters and travellers have used for centuries.

Aulaqut (makes things run away): Designed to startle migrating herds of caribou, these inuksuit were made by piling two or three stones on top of each other and layering heather in between. The heather would blow and dance in the wind, seemingly bringing the inuksuit to life. Frightened, the caribou would try to get away, but the arrangement of the *aulaqut* would lead them right to a group of waiting hunters.

Inuksuk quviasuktuq (inuksuk expressing joy): Whether they are marking good campsites, scenic views, or bountiful hunting zones, these inuksuit serve no real purpose except to signify the pleasure Arctic peoples take in their surroundings.

Niugvaliruluit (that has legs): These inuksuit are used to direct travellers through terrain that is rugged and often has few natural landmarks. Larger *niugvaliruluit* have sighting holes in the centre. They point to other inuksuit far-

Inuksuk quviasuktuq

Niugvaliruluit

Qajakkuviit

ther ahead, thus guiding travellers along the best possible route.

Pirujaqarvik (where the meat cache is): Extra meat from successful hunts would often be left behind, hidden in low spots and covered with stones for retrieval at a later date. These tall towers would mark the spot so these meat caches could be unearthed even once snow and ice had transformed the landscape beyond recognition.

Qajakkuviit (kayak rests): These tall stone towers could often be found at temporary hunting camps. Two built close together would act as a resting place for a kayak, with each tower supporting one end of the overturned vessel. On their own, these inuksuit were useful for keeping meat out of the reach of greedy sled dogs or hungry polar bears.

READING ABOUT...

NEWFOUNDLAND

Kevin Major's novels *Hold Fast* and *Far from Shore* are about Newfoundland kids and families when the island is changing fast. *Blood Red Ochre* is a historical novel about the Beothuks. *The Encyclopedia of Newfoundland* (originated by Joey Smallwood, the former premier) and *The Dictionary of Newfoundland English* tell a lot about Newfoundland history and language.

NOVA SCOTIA

Thomas Raddall wrote many historical novels about Nova Scotia, including *Roger Sudden* and *The Governor's Lady*. More recent novels about the province include *The Baitchopper* by Silver Donald Cameron and *Pit Pony* by Joyce Barkhouse. Helen Creighton collected Nova Scotia ghost stories in *Bluenose Ghosts*.

PRINCE EDWARD ISLAND

The Anne of Green Gables books are famous all over the world, but some readers prefer Lucy Maud Montgomery's other series of novels about an Island girl, Emily of New Moon.

NEW BRUNSWICK

Bliss Carman, one of Canada's first poets, was a New Brunswicker who wrote many poems about his home province. James De Mille was primarily known as a writer of popular adult novels, but he occasionally wrote lovingly about New Brunswick as well.

QUEBEC

Suzanne Martel's *King's Daughter* is a historical novel about New France. Yves Thériault's *Agaguk* is a novel of Inuit life. Brian Doyle's *Up to Low* is set in the Outaouais country, north of Hull.

ONTARIO

Sheila Burnford's *Incredible Journey* is an animal story set in northern Ontario. Janet Lunn's *Root Cellar* and *Shadow in Hawthorn Bay*, Margaret Laurence's *Olden Days Coat*, and Barbara Greenwood's *Days of the Rebels* are all set in the Ontario of the 1800s.

MANITOBA

Scott Young's novels *Scrubs on Skates* and *Boy on Defence* are about kids at a Winnipeg high school. W. D. Valgaardson has written about the Icelandic communities of Manitoba in his books *Thor* and *Sarah and the People of Sand River*. Arthur Slade also draws on Icelandic myths and legends for his Northern Frights series of novels.

SASKATCHEWAN

Maria Campbell wrote *People of the Buffalo* and *Riel's People* to tell young people about her Métis ancestors. Jo Bannatyne-Cugnet's books *A Prairie Alphabet* and *A Prairie Year* have introduced many younger readers to the beauty of the province.

ALBERTA

Sweetgrass by Jan Hudson is a novel about a Blackfoot girl in the years when her people were acquiring guns and horses. The novelist Rudy Wiebe wrote *Alberta: A Celebration*, as well as many other books. Howard and Tamara Palmer wrote *Alberta: A New History*.

BRITISH COLUMBIA

Christy Harris's *Raven's Cry* is a story of the Haida people. Roderick Haig-Brown wrote several B.C. novels for young readers, including *The Whale People* and *Salt-water Summer*. *Boss of the Namko Drive* by Paul St. Pierre is a ranching novel, and the heroine of Joy Kogawa's *Naomi's Road* lives through the deportation of Japanese Canadians during the Second World War.

YUKON

Pierre Berton's history *Klondike* tells the story of the gold rush. Robert Service's popular poems "The Shooting of Dan McGrew" and "The Cremation of Sam McGee" have been beautifully illustrated by the Yukon artist Ted Harrison.

NORTHWEST TERRITORIES

Lost in the Barrens by Farley Mowat is an exciting story about Inuit and non-aboriginal kids who must work together to survive on the Barren Grounds. Fred Bodsworth's *Last of the Curlews*, first published in 1954, is a classic nature story.

NUNAVUT

James Houston has written many young adult books about the Arctic, including *Tikta'liktak*, *The White Archer*, and *Frozen Fire*. Michael Kusugak is the first great Canadian Inuit writer for young people. His books, including *Northern Lights: The Soccer Field* and *A Promise Is a Promise* (co-authored by Robert Munsch), draw on traditional Inuit beliefs and customs.

PHOTO CREDITS

Every reasonable effort has been made to trace the ownership of copyright materials contained in this book. Information enabling the publisher to rectify any reference or credit line in future editions will be welcomed.

Page 13: ©Parks Canada/R. Chipenluk; *14*: B. Brooks/National Film Board/National Archives of Canada (NAC)/PA-154122; *15*: Canadian Press (CP)/Ron Poling; *16*: NAC (Accession No. 1977-14-1); *18*: ©Parks Canada; *20*: NAC/PA-211900; *23*: National Film Board/NAC/PA-128080; *24*: Ken Straiton/First Light.ca; *25*: NAC/C-124432; *26*: NAC/C-143717; *30*: John Sylvester; *31*: ©Parks Canada/J. Pleau; *32*: NAC/C-000939; *34*: NAC/C-002706; *35*: NAC/C-040162; *36*: Fednews telephoto/NAC/PA-177106; *37*: ©Parks Canada/A. Cornellier; *38*: W. R. MacAskill/NAC/PA-030803; *40*: NAC/C-022002; *41*: CP/Albert Lee; *42*: courtesy Bonnie Shemie; *43*: NAC/C-010109; *44*: NAC/C-143714; *48*: Tourism Prince Edward Island/John Sylvester; *50*: G. P. Roberts/NAC/C-000733; *52*: NAC/000810; *54*: Tourism Prince Edward Island/John Sylvester; *55*: Tourism Prince Edward Island/John Sylvester; *56*: John Sylvester; *58*: NAC/PA-127394; *59*: NAC/C-011299; *60*: Tourism Prince Edward Island/John Sylvester; *62*: NAC/143727; *67*: ©Parks Canada/A. F. Helmsley; *69*: courtesy John Martin/Bricklin International; *70*: NAC/C-000168; *72*: ©Parks Canada/C. Reardon; *73*: John Sylvester; *74*: NAC/PA-165626; *77*: William James Topley/NAC/PA-026346; *78*: John Sylvester; *79*: NAC/C-045057; *80*: NAC/C-143719; *85*: ©Parks Canada/J. Beardsell; *86*: NAC/C-006859; *87*: Montreal Gazette/NAC/PA-117477; *88*: CP/Shaney Komulainen; *90*: ©Parks Canada/P. St-Jacques; *91*: ©Parks Canada/J.-F. Bergeron; *93*: NAC/C-019294; *94*: Mac Juster/Montreal Star/NAC/PA-180518; *95*: NAC/PA-209770; *96*: CP/Jacques Boissinot; *97*: CP/Journal de Quebec; *98*: NAC/C-143722; *104*: NAC; *105*: NAC/C-087863; *107*: CP/Toronto Star/Rick Eglinton; *108*: Samuel McLaughlin/NAC/C-000773; *109*: CP/Stratford Beacon Herald/Robin Wilhelm; *111*: CP/London Free Press/Mike Hensen; *112*: CP; *114*: CP/Frank Gunn; *115*: Notman & Fraser/NAC/PA-028631; *116*: NAC/C-143718; *120*: ©Parks Canada/R. Beardmore; *122*: NAC/PA-012854; *124*: Hudson's Bay Company, Provincial Archives of Manitoba, P-181 (H. Jones, *A Souteaux Indian, Travelling with His Family Near Lake Winnipeg*); *126*: Provincial Archives of Manitoba–Winnipeg–Streets–Main 1882 1 (N16067); *127*: ©Parks Canada/P. McCloskey; *128*: ©Parks Canada/W. Lynch; *130*: Glenbow Archives NA-4868-211; *132*: CP/Adrian Wyld; *133*: NAC/C-055449; *134*: NAC/C-143723; *138*: courtesy Courtney Milne; *140*: Glenbow Archives NA-98-12; *141*: Glenbow Archives ND-3-6742; *142*: O. B. Buell/NAC/PA-118768; *144*: CP/Jacques Boissinot; *145*: NAC/C-002424; *146*: CP/Regina Leader Post/Roy Antal; *148*: Glenbow Archives NA-1063-1; *149*: Glenbow Archives NA-2310-1; *150*: CP/Adrian Wyld; *151*: O. B. Buell/NAC/C-001873; *152*: NAC/C-143724; *157*: NAC/C-097667; *158*: Glenbow Archives NA-919-48; *159*: Glenbow Archives NA-789-80; *161*: Glenbow Archives NA-3981-15; *162*: CP/Adrian Wyld; *163* (top): Glenbow Archives NA-2308-1; *163* (bottom): NAC/C-000403; *164*: CP/Jeff McIntosh; *167*: Glenbow Archives NA-263-1; *168*: courtesy Bonnie Shemie; *170*: NAC/C-143720; *176*: NAC/C-003693; *178*: Glenbow Archives NA-3740-29; *179*: NAC/C-029464; *180*: CP/Victoria Times-Colonist/Ray Smith; *181*: Trevor Bonderud/First Light.ca; *183*: CP/Chuck Stoody; *185*: Glenbow Archives NA-654-6; *186*: First Light.ca; *188*: NAC/C-143721; *192*: ©Parks Canada/W. Lynch; *193*: ©Parks Canada/W. Lynch; *194*: Seattle, Wash. LaRoche/NAC/C-28652; *196*: Glenbow Archives NA-1864-23; *198*: Chris Harris/First Light.ca; *199*: Larss and Duclos/NAC/C-006648; *201*: ©Parks Canada/W. Lynch; *202*: J. Doody/NAC/C-003070; *203*: William James Topley/NAC/PA-033761; *204*: Ken Straiton/First Light.ca; *206*: NAC/C-148927; *211*: LANDSAT data © NOAA. Received by the Canada Centre for Remote Sensing (CCRS). Processed and distributed by RADARSAT under licence from CCRS; *213*: CP/Kevin Frayer; *214*: NAC/PA-017946; *215*: NAC/C-040372; *216*: CP/Chuck Stoody; *218*: CP/Bob Green; *220*: courtesy Professor Owen Beattie, University of Alberta; *221*: NAC/C-002146; *222*: CP/Chuck Stoody; *224*: NAC/C-143725; *228*: ©Parks Canada/G. Klassen; *229*: NAC/C-014073; *230*: © Bettman/CORBIS; *233*: NAC/C-032708; *234*: CP/Jonathan Hayward; *237*: NAC/PA-193047; *240*: courtesy Daniel Kreuger/Nunavut Tourism; *241*: courtesy Daniel Kreuger/Nunavut Tourism; *242*: Department of Canadian Heritage.

INDEX